# Self-Advocacy Skills for Students with Learning Disabilities

## Making It Happen In College and Beyond

### Henry B. Reiff, Ph.D.

DUDE
PUBLISHING

DUDE PUBLISHING
A Division of
National Professional Resources, Inc.
Port Chester, New York

**Publisher's Cataloging-in-Publication**
*(Provided by Quality Books, Inc.)*

Reiff, Henry B., 1953-
    Self-advocacy skills for students with learning
disabilities : making it happen in college and beyond /
Henry B. Reiff.
    p. cm.
    Includes bibliographical references.
    ISBN-13: 978-1-934032-06-0
    ISBN-10: 1-934032-06-9

    1. Learning disabled--Education (Higher)--United
States.  2. Learning disabled--Services for--United
States.  3. Self-help techniques.  4. Autonomy
(Psychology)    I. Title.

    LC4818.38.R45 2007                    371.92'6
                                    QBI07-600029

Acquisitions Editor: Helene M. Hanson
Associate Editor: Lisa L. Hanson
Production Editor, Cover Design: Andrea Cerone,
National Professional Resources, Inc., Port Chester, NY

© 2007 Henry B. Reiff

Dude Publishing
A Division of National Professional Resources, Inc.
25 South Regent Street
Port Chester, New York 10573
Toll free: (800) 453-7461
Phone: (914) 937-8879

Visit our web site: www.NPRinc.com

Printed in the United States of America

ISBN 978-1-934032-06-0

*This book is dedicated to my family — my wife, Jacki, and my children, Benjamin and Chandra — who make it happen everyday.*

## Table of Contents

Acknowledgements ............................................................ I

Introduction ............................................................. III

Prologue .............................................................. IX

Chapter 1 ~ Getting There .................................... 1

Self-Advocacy and Transition Planning for College ..................... 1

  Self-Advocacy and the IEP .............................................. 1
  Understanding Strengths and Weakensses ............................ 3
  Getting the Documentation Colleges Want ........................... 4
    Exhibit 1.1. Documentation for Colleges............................ 6
    Exhibit 1.2. Differences Between IDEA and ADA ............. 8
    Exhibit 1.3. Obstacles to Getting the Documentation
                   Colleges May Require ..................................... 9
  Transition Planning Year by Year ...................................... 9

Things to Know Before Applying ................................. 14

  Criteria for Admission ................................................... 14
    Exhibit 1.4. Questions for the Application and Admission Process ... 15
  Services ................................................................... 15
  Size and Location ....................................................... 16
  General Atmosphere ................................................... 21

Tips for Students ................................................ 26

  It's Never too Early to Get Serious About College ..................... 26
  How to Learn More About Yourself ................................... 27
  What to Do When You Visit a College ................................ 30
  Filling out Your Application ............................................ 31
    Exhibit 1.5. Tips for Writing the Admissions Essay .............. 35
  Friendly Advice from a Dean of Admissions ......................... 36

Tips for Parents ................................................ 37

  If You Enable, Your Child May Be Unable ............................ 37
  The IEP — Where Do You Fit In? Where Do You Stay Out?.............. 40
    Exhibit 1.6. Tips for Parents at IEP Meetings.................... 43
  Cost, or How Will We Ever Pay for This? ........................... 43
  Filling out Financial Aid Forms ....................................... 47
    Exhibit 1.7. Tips for Financial Aid .............................. 48

Tips for Guidance Counselors .......................................... 49
   Promoting Self-Awareness and Self-Advocacy ........................... 49
   Your Role in the IEP ................................................. 50
      Exhibit 1.8. Five Questions Guidance Counselors Should
                   Ask at IEP Meetings .................................. 51
   Course Selection in High School ...................................... 51
   Kinds of Academic Programs Offered: An Unabashed Endorsement .... 52

Chapter 2 ~ Staying There: Self-Advocacy in College ....... 59

Three Things to Know ..................................................... 59
   What the Law Does and Doesn't Provide ................................ 59
   How to Use Disability Services ....................................... 63
      Exhibit 2.1. Student Questions for Initial Meeting with DS ........... 65
   Deciphering Psychoeducational Evaluations ............................ 69

Goal Planning ............................................................ 78
      Exhibit 2.2. Goal Planning Program — Spring 2006 ................ 83
      Exhibit 2.3. Progress in Courses .................................... 84

Developing and Building Study Skills .................................... 85
   You Gotta Have a Plan, Stan .......................................... 85
   Planning and Organization ............................................ 87
      Exhibit 2.4. Daily-Weekly Schedule .................................. 93
      Exhibit 2.5. Jason's Daily Schedule ................................. 95
   A Home Away from Home ................................................ 99
   Keep it all in Perspective ........................................... 101
   In Class ............................................................. 102
   Out of Class ......................................................... 109
   How to Study ......................................................... 113
   Taking Tests ......................................................... 118
   Writing Papers ....................................................... 125
   The Age of Assistive Technology ...................................... 132

Tips for Students ........................................................ 136
   Stand Up for Your Right(s) ........................................... 136
   Understanding Your Learning Disabilities ............................. 138
   Keeping it Together .................................................. 142
   Want Pizza and Beer? Get a Job ....................................... 143

Tips for Parents ................................................ 149

Flying the Helicopter .............................................. 149
Paying for Assistive Technology — Hi Tech at Lo Cost ................... 152
Mom, Dad — Send Money ........................................... 153

Tips for Guidance Counselors ............................... 154

Promoting Self-Advocacy in College ................................ 154
Translating Psychobabble ........................................... 156
Paving the Way for Future Students ................................ 160
Lurking on the Listserv ............................................ 165

Chapter 3 ~ Making It In The World Beyond ............... 167

Is Grad School in the Future? .............................. 167

It's Better the Second Time Around ............................... 167
LD Support Programs in Graduate and Professional Schools ......... 168
Consider This ................................................... 170

Self-Advocacy — The Gift that Keeps on Giving .......... 173

It's Never Too Late to Learn ..................................... 173
Stand Up for Your Right(s) — Again! .............................. 175
Making a First Impression That's not the Last Impression ............. 178
Social Skills in the Workplace .................................... 180

Finding the Road to Success When You Can't
Read the Directions ........................................ 184

Successful Adults With Learning Disabilities ...................... 184

Accommodations in the Workplace ......................... 187

What the Law Says .............................................. 187
Determining Reasonable Accommodations ........................ 188

There's More to Life Than Work ........................... 191

What Is Success? ................................................ 191
Life 101 ....................................................... 193

Tips for Students .......................................... 196

To Disclose or Not to Disclose — That is the Question ................ 196
Pick Your Battles ............................................... 198
If You Do What You Love, You'll Love What You Do ................... 199

Tips for Parents .................................................... 201
    They Grow Up So Fast — Or Not Fast Enough ............................. 201
    Keeping the Empty Nest Empty ................................................ 202
Tips for Guidance Counselors ...................................... 204
    Career Planning in High School for the College-Bound .................... 204
    Getting Your Students to Think About the Next Seventy Years ........ 206
Resources ........................................................... 209

### *Acknowledgements*

The author would like to acknowledge the following people who were instrumental in making this book a reality:

Dr. Paul Gerber, my mentor and friend who has guided my career from the beginning;

Dr. Rick Ginsberg, who completed our research team;

Helene Hanson at National Professional Resources, Inc. who transformed a manuscript into a book;

and most of all, the students with whom I have worked at McDaniel College.

## Introduction

Why is self-advocacy so important? Most of us do not see individuals with learning disabilities as second class citizens in a colonized imperial state. But in some profound ways, it may not be all that different. Our society prides itself on the metaphor of a melting pot, a cauldron that blends different ingredients together until they become one thing. We value sameness. We value the norm. Our educational system is more concerned with holding up the norm as the goal rather than affirming individuality. If you are someone with learning disabilities, you are different. You deviate from the norm. By definition, you are a statistical outlier. We live in a world of "disability apartheid," a place where our cultural, social, and political values and assumptions unwittingly tend to deny people with disabilities their most fundamental right to be themselves. Much of formal education attempts to make students with learning disabilities less different, more like everyone else, more like the norm. I don't know about you, but I don't aspire to shooting for the middle. Mediocrity is not my goal. I'll reach for the stars, thank you. And the only way I can do that is to be me.

Self-advocacy is all about being me...or you. As you will see in this book, it begins simply with recognition of being different. From that recognition can come acceptance, understanding, and eventually a sense of how to work with one's unique strengths and weaknesses, how to work with the system, how to challenge it when necessary, how to ask for and get help while being as independent, autonomous, and individual as possible. It's a tall order, but it's not impossible. When high school students with learning disabilities ask me for advice about college and beyond, my reply usually begins like this:

> Come into my office. Let's talk about college and what comes after. Have you thought about where you want to go? What are you going to do when you get there? Do you think you can make it? Are you scared? That's OK — it's only natural. The good news is, thousands of college students with learning disabilities graduate every year and go on to lead successful, satisfying lives. But it's not easy. You'll have to work hard. And it's not like high school. Nobody's going to make sure you have an Individualized Education Program (IEP). You'll have to speak up for yourself. You have to make it happen.

Not too many years ago, the idea that students with learning disabilities would routinely be attending traditional colleges and universities seemed pretty far-fetched. Today, however, students with learning disabilities are a fixture in most, if not all institutions of higher learning. The number of college students with learning disabilities has more than doubled since 1985; students with learning disabilities comprise almost five percent of the college population. Many of these students are invisible, at least in terms of having learning disabilities. They've decided, as is their right, not to tell anyone about their learning disabilities, and they manage completely on their own. Many others, however, advocate for themselves as students with learning disabilities. Most of these students use some degree of support to help them be successful in college. Almost all colleges and universities now provide special support and services to students with learning disabilities.

In addition to traditional four-year undergraduate programs, high school students with learning disabilities have a whole range of postsecondary options, from community college to vocational training, including highly specialized technical training. Although this guide offers information that should be useful for all students, it is aimed primarily at helping students with learning disabilities who are hoping or planning to attend a traditional four-year college or university. Many students, their parents, and even some guidance counselors are concerned that the competition to get into college is so fierce that students with learning disabilities need not apply. Don't buy into this myth. Although a handful of elite institutions accept a miniscule proportion of applicants, most colleges and universities accept the *majority* of students who apply. There is a college out there for virtually any student with learning disabilities who wants to go, as long as that student is serious, motivated, and reads this book!

In my thirty-year career as a teacher, professor, dean, and consultant, I've had hundreds, or maybe thousands, of conversations with students about getting into college, staying in, and making it in life. I imagined this book as one of those conversations — except longer! As I wrote, I could picture a student sitting across from me. As I put my thoughts down on paper, however, I realized that I sometimes was seeing the student's parents in the room and talking to them as well. Finally, I began to imagine similar conversations with guidance counselors. It is somewhat daunting for students with learning disabilities to consider going to college and making it in life. Having a strong, knowledgeable, and skilled support team of parents and guidance counselors makes that journey easier to navigate.

Working together as a team usually beats trying to go it alone.

The purpose of this book is to provide students with learning disabilities, their parents, and guidance counselors with effective strategies to encourage and develop self-advocacy skills that will benefit them from high school to college and into the world beyond. I will individually address the key players: students, parents, and guidance counselors. You are all invited to my office for a chat. Because I want to speak with each of you individually, I include three sections, one each for students, parents, and guidance counselors, at the end of each chapter of the book. It would be odd, even alarming, if I gave completely different advice to each group. We're all on the same team. In some cases, I pick up on issues previously discussed and go into details that I think are particularly relevant for each group. To some extent, you might notice a degree of redundancy from one section to another. However, you may still want to take a look at the other sections. Students, you'll want to know what I'm telling your parents and guidance counselors. Parents, you'll want to know what I'm telling your kids. And guidance counselors, well, you like knowing everything.

This book should also prove useful to secondary special education and general education teachers, college admissions personnel, postsecondary disability services providers, and other professionals and paraprofessionals. It answers questions students have about college while giving parents and educators insights and practical tools for proactive planning. This is a guide that students, parents, guidance counselors, and anyone interested in college students with learning disabilities should share with one another.

My hope is that this book will be a companion for students with learning disabilities, much as *The Lonely Planet Guide to Thailand* was to me during a month-long trip to that country some years ago. Before I had even purchased plane tickets, I studied the book, got a general feel for the country, set up an itinerary, and dreamed about what I would see. Once I got to Thailand, I kept the book by my side. It navigated me through large cities and small towns; it gave me Thai phrases that would help with traveling, eating, and shopping; it took me off the beaten path to new discoveries. At night, I would often reread descriptions of places I had just visited to compare observations. That guide kept me grounded when I was in a new, strange, and challenging place, and most importantly, it allowed me to be more independent. It gave me the skills I needed to advocate for myself in a new, different, and exciting world. Learning to be an effective self-advocate in a strange land took some work. I had prepared before I left. I referred to the guide constantly while I was traveling. There were some rough spots, and every now and then even the book couldn't help me — I had to use my own wits. The guide was a constant reminder that others just like me had negotiated getting around in a foreign land; with that book, I knew I could, too. When it was over, I'd had the trip of a lifetime. I still like looking at that guide. It was my companion. I hope that this book, *Self-Advocacy Skills for Students with Learning Disabilities: Making It Happen in College and Beyond,* will be your companion to help navigate through the post-secondary years.

## Prologue

In my opinion, Bob Marley was the greatest musical force of the twentieth century. The fact that he created and popularized a genre of music that has seeped into virtually every type of music around the world has made him an icon. But what makes him such an extraordinary phenomenon is that he believed his music could change lives, locally and globally. He opened up his home outside Kingston and fed thousands of Jamaica's poorest on a daily basis. He made change happen.

More like Martin Luther King than Luther Vandross, Bob Marley's passionate advocacy for human rights magnetically attracted opposing political parties in Jamaica, encouraging them to work together. And because he was a true advocate for the oppressed and downtrodden, he rejected the corruption of the politicians who courted him, which resulted in an assassination attempt and a self-imposed exile in England. At a point when he could have gracefully retired into rock star affluence and indulgence, he broadened his commitment to advocate for marginalized peoples all over the world. He believed in the inherent rights of all humanity. His message was simple, his spirit irresistible:

> *Get Up! Stand Up!*
> *Stand Up for Your Right.*
> *Get Up! Stand Up!*
> *Don't Give Up the Fight.*[1]

What does Bob Marley have to do with students with learning disabilities who want to get into college, stay in,

---

[1] Peter Tosh & Bob Marley, 1977.

and make it in life? Successful persons with learning disabilities have characteristics in common that have allowed them to be successful. They were all skilled self-advocates. They got up and stood up for their rights. Bob Marley did not tell people that he would take care of them. He did not say that he would stand up for their rights. Instead, his message was that everyone has to take care of themselves, that he would support them but that they needed...to get up and stand up.

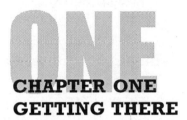

# CHAPTER ONE
# GETTING THERE

## Self-Advocacy and Transition Planning for College

### Self-Advocacy and the IEP

Students who have been identified as having learning disabilities, as well as their parents and their guidance counselors, are undoubtedly familiar with the Individual Education Program (IEP), the document that helps determine the student's long-term goals, short-term objectives, and the services necessary to achieve them. By the time the student is fourteen years old — sixteen at the latest — the IEP should include something called a statement of needed transition services. These services involve a coordinated set of activities that help the student prepare for post-high school experiences, including going to college. In order to develop this transition plan, the members of the IEP team (usually a special education teacher, general education teacher, administrator, and other school personnel) should

1

schedule a meeting with the student and parent(s). I recommend that the college guidance counselor from the high school also get involved at this stage.

In some schools, this process will proceed smoothly and the team will invite the student and parent(s) to meet to begin this process of transition planning within the first two years of high school; however, this is not always the case. Although the Individuals with Disabilities Education Act of 1990 (IDEA, PL 101-476) and the newest reauthorization, the Individuals with Disabilities Education Improvement Act of 2004 (PL 108-446, often known as IDEA 2004), mandate transition planning, the law allows each school a great deal of flexibility in the way in which this planning occurs.

It may be necessary for students with learning disabilities, their families, and/or guidance counselors, to initiate transition planning, specifically for transition to college. The student may need to bring up the matter with the coordinator of the IEP team, usually a special education teacher. If the student isn't sure who heads the team, any teacher or administrator should be able to help. As much as this book is about self-advocacy, this is a time when parents or guidance counselors may be quite helpful, particularly by encouraging the student to look into transition planning and, when necessary, by running some interference along the way.

The team should begin by working with the student to determine the kinds of skills, knowledge, and competencies needed to enter college. Different colleges have different requirements, so it's essential to have an idea of what type of college the student is planning to attend. Whether it's a local community college, a nearby commuter branch of the state university system, the flagship campus of the state university, a traditional (and usually private) liberal arts institution, a technical college, or some other specialized program, entrance requirements will be different for each. The team should help determine what kind of preparation is necessary.

## Understanding Strengths and Weaknesses

Once the team has an idea of the type of post-secondary education the student is considering, it's time to assess and understand the student's strengths, weaknesses, and needs. Figuring these out will be different in each individual circumstance. This is obviously not a one-size-fits-all process. Because it's highly individualized, transition planning for college presents a logical and timely opportunity to conduct a comprehensive psychoeducational assessment and evaluation, as the results may clarify some of the learning issues previously identified.

Typically, an evaluation of learning disabilities will include results from both aptitude/ability tests (intelligence) and achievement tests (grade level in different subjects). A thoughtful evaluation of the student's scores on ability testing (usually the WISC, the WAIS, or the Woodcock-Johnson Cognitive Battery) will help build a better understanding of the student's overall learning style. Achievement test results will pinpoint academic strengths and weaknesses. These scores may provide a rough blueprint of areas that require special attention or tutoring. They may help the team determine whether the student should look into college programs that waive or accommodate foreign language or math requirements.

If the IEP team is especially focused on superior college transition planning, or if the student, parents, and guidance counselor can advocate forcefully, assessment and evaluation may incorporate additional measures and instruments particularly relevant to the unique demands of college. For example, as much as ability and achievement tests may reveal insights about learning style, an instrument such as the Learning Style Inventory (LSI) provides more specific diagnostic information. Numerous students have told me that they never really learned how to study in high school, often because they did not need to! But study skills are vitally important to college success. A measure such as the Learning and Study Skills Inventory (LASSI) specifically assesses how a student studies. If meeting foreign language requirements is likely to present overwhelming difficulties, results from the Modern Language Aptitude Test (MLAT) may provide convincing evidence that a waiver or substitution is in order.

## Getting the Documentation Colleges Want

The timeliness of comprehensive testing has recently become critical. Many colleges and universities with programs for students with learning disabilities now require documentation based on a formal evaluation administered within three years of applying. Up until 1997, federal law (IDEA, 1990) required IEP testing every three years. Consequently, a student with documented learning disabilities would receive an evaluation automatically within three years of going to college; however, recent reauthorizations (IDEA '97 [P.L. 105-17] and the current IDEA 2004) no longer mandate triennial evaluations. Subsequently, students, their parents, and guidance counselors may need to advocate for updated testing. If the student plans to receive services at college and does not have updated testing (usually within the last two years of high school), the family may have to arrange for a private evaluation, an increasingly pricey process ($500 - $2,000+). On the other hand, if the transition plan states that the college applications require current documentation, the plan should provide for new testing before graduation. I cannot overemphasize the importance of advocating for these services. If someone does not speak up, getting current testing may be overlooked.

Colleges and universities don't use one standard set of documentation. However, the majority of schools follow guidelines developed by the Association for Higher Education And Disability (AHEAD). Most institutions will ask for evaluations that use both ability and achievement tests. Exhibit 1.1 shows the most commonly accepted tests, as well as some that are unlikely to be accepted.

## Exhibit 1.1. Documentation for Colleges

*Commonly Accepted Ability Tests*

> **WAIS: Wechsler Adult Intelligence Scale** — the "gold standard" for colleges and universities
> **WJ-COG: Woodcock-Johnson Tests of Cognitive Abilities** — accepted by most schools that accept the WAIS
> **SB: Stanford-Binet** — an old workhorse, probably acceptable but not as commonly used as the WAIS and WJ
> **KAAIT: Kaufman Adolescent and Adult Intelligence Test** — contemporary, but not as commonly used as the WAIS and WJ
> **WISC: Wechsler Intelligence Scale for Children** — if it's the most recent testing, it's probably too old or inappropriate for a high school student

*Commonly Accepted Achievement Tests*

> **WJ-ACH: Woodcock-Johnson Tests of Achievement** — the achievement tests students are most likely to be given
> **WIAT or WIAT-II: Wechsler Individual Achievement Test** — more likely from a private evaluation
> **ND: Nelson-Denny Reading Test** — often part of the package from diagnoses of dyslexia
> **SATA: Scholastic Abilities Test for Adults** — newer test, not common but probably accepted

*Tests to Avoid (not commonly accepted by colleges)*

> **WRAT: Wide Range Achievement Test** — not recommended in the AHEAD guidelines because it's not a comprehensive measure
> **K-BIT: Kaufman Brief Intelligence Test** — not a comprehensive measure
> **SIT-R: Slosson Intelligence Test-Revised** — also not a comprehensive measure

Here's something that may come as a shock: *A diagnosis of Learning Disabilities in public school is not a legally binding determination at the college level that a learning disability exists* (Hatzes, Reiff, & Bramel, 2002). IDEA 2004 applies to grades K-12, but not to college. At the post-secondary level, the Americans with Disabilities Act (ADA) comes into play. Colleges will not automatically provide support services or even consider a student learning disabled just because that student qualified for special education services while in elementary and/or secondary school. Denial of services isn't the norm; but because the ADA defines a disability as *substantially limiting* one or more major life activities, disability service providers at the college and university level may determine that a student isn't substantially limited and consequently does not qualify for services, particularly if ADD has been the only diagnosis. College is different than high school. The change from IDEA to ADA is part of this brave new world.

**Exhibit 1.2. Differences Between IDEA and ADA**

| <u>IDEA 2004</u> | <u>ADA</u> |
|---|---|
| **Entitlement Act**<br>*Entitles* individuals with disabilities from the age of 3 through 21 to free, appropriate public education in the least restrictive environment. | **Civil Rights Statute**<br>"Levels the playing field" for qualified individuals who meet the criteria of disability, defined as a physical or mental impairment that *substantially limits* one or more major life activities. |
| **Who qualifies for services?**<br>Any student identified by the school system as LD. | **Who qualifies for services?**<br>ADA defines disability differently than IDEA. A student with LD in high school may not be considered LD in some colleges. |
| **How are services obtained?**<br>Student is evaluated through school system; LD diagnosis ensures IEP. | **How are services obtained?**<br>Students with LD are required to provide institutions with documentation that verifies their disability. |
| **What are the services?**<br>Individualized Education Program (IEP) is mandated once the student qualifies as LD. | **What are the services?**<br>Equal access to education programs and nonacademic services for qualified individuals. |
| **How often is testing required?**<br>Testing every three years is not required. | **How often is testing required?**<br>Many colleges require testing administered no more than three years prior to admission. |

Most students with learning disabilities who seek special services in college are successful. To facilitate this process, students, parents, and counselors should be proactive and aware of potential obstacles and challenges to getting appropriate services in college.

---

**Exhibit 1.3. Obstacles to Getting the Documentation Colleges May Require**

**The following should be carefully considered when compiling documentation:**

1. Inconsistency across institutions regarding documentation requirements;

2. Uncertainty regarding who qualifies as an individual with a disability;

3. Inadequacy of documentation as it relates to meeting institutional guidelines;

4. Misperceptions among students, parents, and guidance counselors (not to mention special education teachers, school psychologists, and postsecondary disability service providers) that the services and accommodations received at the elementary and secondary levels will automatically carry over into the postsecondary setting.

---

## Transition Planning Year by Year

For the college-bound student, transition planning should include academic preparation guided by college preparatory coursework, goal setting, study skill assessment and development, and personal and social skill development. The process involves a team effort in which the student is an active participant, and the transition team case manager coordinates activities and ensures follow through. If done effectively, transition planning should improve self-understanding and promote self-advocacy skills. The ultimate goal of transition planning for college-bound students with learning disabilities is to choose a college that matches well with the student's strengths, weaknesses, needs, and interests.

When should transition planning start? What is the actual process? Although there is no single answer, a transition project from North Dakota furnishes a useful set of general guidelines (http://www.dpi.state.nd.us/transitn/secspec.shtm). I have adapted these guidelines specifically for students who are thinking about attending college or university.

### Eighth and Ninth Grade: Getting on Track

An eighth-grade *career portfolio* may help the student start thinking about the types of education necessary for preparing for different careers. This is also the time to start a *college portfolio* that should include articles, pictures, and brochures of colleges that may be of interest. Exploring college and university websites is another good source of information. The IEP team meeting this year should include some discussion about long-range planning, including some consideration of financial planning. As the student, parents, and team are now thinking about life after high school, this meeting provides an ideal opportunity to outline a four-year transition plan that will serve as an integral part of the IEP. This process should be continued and updated in ninth grade, by which time the team should have a pretty good idea of the types of courses the student will be taking in high school.

Students who are college bound need to take a college preparatory curriculum. I encourage students to take honors courses in high school, beginning in ninth grade. Admissions officers *love* honors courses. Students with learning disabilities are frequently intimidated by the very idea of an honors class, in many cases because teachers, advisors, or counselors discourage them from undertaking this challenge. Honors courses are not necessarily harder than non-honors courses. Because they are usually smaller, students can get more individual attention. Students with learning disabilities who advocate for themselves may be able to help teachers of honors classes focus on what they can do rather than what they cannot.

### Tenth Grade: Learning About College

By grade ten, it's time to start collecting catalogs and admissions material from colleges — and not only first choice colleges. There are an incredible number of colleges out there that you probably have never heard of, and one of them may be the perfect match! Guides to colleges and universities, such as *Peterson's College Guide* (also available online at http://www.petersons.com) and *Lovejoy's College Guide,* give a fair amount of information about a wide variety of schools. Some guides, such as *K & W Guide to Colleges for the Learning Disabled, Peterson's Colleges with Programs for Students with Learning Disabilities or Attention Deficit Disorder*, and *Lovejoy's College Guide for the Learning Disabled,* specifically review colleges with programs for students with learning disabilities. Don't get too hung up on the rankings in *U.S. News and World Report*; while they give ballpark information, these rankings rely on institutional data and don't necessarily describe what day-to-day life is all about. In fact, the best insights may come from publications that do in-depth research including interviews with students, alumni, and teachers. Loren Pope has provided just this kind of research in the books *Looking Beyond the Ivy League: Finding the College That's Right for You*, and *Colleges That Change Lives: 40 Schools You Should Know About Even If You're Not A Straight-A Student.* Joe Anne Adler also offers guidance in the book *100 Colleges Where Average Students*

*Can Excel.* These books explore lesser known, smaller colleges and universities that, in many cases, have made a commitment to working with students with learning disabilities.

The IEP team should now have a pretty good idea of the courses required for admission to the type of school that interests the student. In tenth grade, the team should encourage the student to take these courses, and should include additional preparation and support for courses that are likely to be difficult. Finally, all previous plans should be updated; if available, a yearly IEP meeting is the logical place to conduct this review.

### Eleventh Grade: Tests and Road Trips

Grade eleven is really the beginning of the college admissions process. Those dreaded admissions tests, the SAT and the ACT, loom ahead. How can a student with learning disabilities prepare? A number of services claim that taking their prep class can increase SAT scores by 100 points. While it's clear that good test-taking skills are an asset on standardized tests, the makers of the SAT refute the claims of prep classes and contend that they are unlikely to result in significant improvement. Nevertheless, many students with learning disabilities fare poorly on standardized tests, in many cases because they don't use the same test-taking skills employed by most students: They don't develop a logical plan for ruling out unlikely answers; they don't read the questions carefully; they don't skip troublesome questions with a strategy of coming back after answering the others; they don't have a method of making reasonable guesses, etc. Consequently, depending on the test-taking abilities of the student, I do recommend individualized preparation, which may include an SAT prep course. Students with learning disabilities can learn to become better test takers.

Eleventh grade is also the time to start looking at specific colleges more thoroughly. It's important to move beyond printed material and begin talking to people connected with colleges. Take advantage of local college fairs, as they generally offer the opportunity to meet admissions counselors and ask questions face-to-face. Making this personal connection can help provide a better sense of the intangibles, such as the "feel" of the learning disabilities support program, but remember that admissions counselors are in the business of selling their institution. Therefore, students should ask the admissions counselor for names of alumni who can talk to them about the college. Once again, alumni will not necessarily present the most objective perspective, but they do provide additional insight. In particular, be attuned to consistency or a lack thereof in what you hear about the school. Just because everyone says the same things about an institution does not necessarily make it true, but it does tend to increase credibility. On the other hand, conflicting viewpoints should raise some red flags. In either case, information at this level should lead to questions and issues to explore when visiting colleges or universities.

### Twelfth Grade: Applications and Decisions

The goal of transition planning in twelfth grade should be for the student to apply, be accepted by, and commit to a college or university by spring of this school year. Before the year is out, the student will have embarked on a major new phase of education and life. Consequently, senior year really is one of transition.

At this time, students (and their parents and guidance counselors) who have followed through on all the preceding suggestions may not only feel ready for college, but ready for the diploma! Of course, the work isn't over yet. Now begins the application process. Many students report that they receive dozens of college brochures weekly; most brochures make any college look pretty attractive, so it's important to do some homework. Students cannot apply to every college they hear about. Applications are time consuming, and with processing fees, the expense will rise quickly. Five or six well-made choices should be sufficient.

Perhaps the most important element to consider when making final selections is goodness-of-fit. Does the school offer educational opportunities that will allow the student to make full use of strengths, provide accommodations and support for areas of weakness, and generally address and meet individual needs? No two students are alike. No two colleges are alike either. The more the students know about themselves and the colleges, the better the match will be.

## Things to Know Before Applying

### Criteria for Admission

I cannot provide all of the information that is needed about applying to college. Each individual situation is different. Instead, I'll try to help outline the right questions. Let's begin by reviewing the checklist of questions and considerations presented in Exhibit 1.4.

**Exhibit 1.4. Questions for the Application and Admission Process**

**Consider the appropriateness of applying to a particular college based upon answers to questions such as the following:**

- Does the college being considered require minimum SAT/ACT scores and/or minimum GPA?
- Are applicants with learning disabilities who don't meet minimum standards considered?
- Does the college calculate all grades or only college preparatory coursework in determining high school grade point average?
- What is the impact of special education, developmental, or skill-building courses taken in high school?
- Has the student taken the types of courses suggested by the college?

## Services

As previously stated, special services for students with disabilities, learning as well as other, are available in higher education institutions. But the nature and scope of these services vary under the broad heading of disability services (DS). Consequently, it is important to know just what kind(s) of learning disabilities services each college provides. Consider the following five-point continuum model developed by Dr. Stan Shaw and his associates at the University of Connecticut[2]:

Level 1: No services available — rare but possible

Level 2: Decentralized and limited services — extended

---

[2] See Shaw, S.F., McGuire, J.M., & Brinckerhoff, L.C. (1994). College and university programming. In P.J. Gerber & H.B. Reiff (Eds.), Learning Disabilities in Adulthood (pp. 141-151). Austin, TX: PRO-ED.

time might be provided; other support is minimal

Level 3: Loosely coordinated services — accommodations may be available in one class but not another

Level 4: Centrally coordinated services — the institution has made a commitment to disability services and has a special office and program

Level 5: Databased services — cutting edge, usually connected to a graduate program in special education

## Size and Location

### *Big or Small?*

Colleges and universities range in size from a few hundred students to more than fifty thousand. A college may be smaller than an elementary school or larger than a small city. Generally, smaller schools provide more individualized contact with faculty and staff. Many small colleges pride themselves on classes that average twenty or fewer students (probably even smaller than elementary school), taught primarily by full-time faculty. At this size school, students have the opportunity to get to know their professors on an individual and often personal level. If the school also has a comprehensive support program for students with learning disabilities, it's likely that staff in the disability office will know something about professors and often have an existing working relationship with them. The program staff will also get to know the student with learning disabilities. In many small colleges, a student simply cannot hide! Professionals from all walks of campus life take an interest in students and their needs. Even on a small campus, however, the student has to seek support, an initial step of self-advocacy.

So what's not to like about a small college? Some students simply don't want to be in such a setting. They want the excitement, the energy, and perhaps even the anonymity of being part of a small city of college students. Certainly a drawback to smaller schools is they don't have the stuff — cool and otherwise — found at State U, not to mention large and usually prestigious private universities. Small colleges may offer intimacy but not stadiums packed with 80,000 rabid fans on fall afternoons, frequent concerts from national headliners, a mile-long fraternity row, count-less coffee houses, bars, clubs, bookstores, cheap late-night eats, and so on. Larger institutions also tend to have more resources and services. A support program for students with learning disabilities may be non-existent in many of the smaller schools. A large university probably has technologi-cal and other resources that small schools can only dream about. The trade off, however, is often classes with 500 other students, where the closest contact the student has with the professor is on the video monitor in the auditorium.

At a big university, there is a lot of cool stuff, but it may be hard to find or not always available. That beautiful workout facility? Sorry, it's for football players only. The big concert at the university arena? Wow, it sold out in two hours. That new coffee house across campus? Whoops, got lost trying to find it. Students with learning disabilities who are thinking about attending a large school should have strong self-advocacy skills and a working understanding of their personal strengths, weaknesses, and needs. The LD support program may be huge, but if the student does not take the following measures, support services will not be very useful:

- Seek out specific support,
- Make her/himself known,
- Know how to tell someone what kinds of accommodations are needed in specific classes,
- Know what kinds of classes are likely to be hard or easy,
- Follow up to make sure people are doing what they say they'll do.

Of course, at many universities the situation is much different. Some support services for students with learning disabilities have surprisingly low staff-to-student ratios, allowing students to easily build personal and productive relationships with staff. Because larger programs generally have more highly trained staff, professional experts in learning disabilities often help students discover a great deal about their learning styles and guide them in making sound decisions about types of courses to take and accommodations to request. Staff at many service programs are strong advocates for their students and closely monitor their welfare.

Even with a solid support program, other obstacles exist in large universities. In a class of 500 students, the professor is unlikely to be aware of a student's name, much less how that student learns best. For many students with learning disabilities, the scenario of anonymously bobbing in a sea of hundreds of classmates, sitting through an hour or more of nothing but lecture from a faraway face peering out from behind a lectern, having no interaction, no discussion, no involvement except staying quiet and taking notes, is hardly ideal.

Of course, large classes can provide effective learning experiences. Many professors take a great deal of pride in being excellent teachers and incorporate technological wizardry that rivals that of Disney World into their lessons. But no matter the pyrotechnics in the classroom, these classes still lack a personal touch. It's less likely that the professor at a large university will have a personal working relationship with support services for students with learning disabilities. As far as how the class itself is put together, the student with learning disabilities is no different from anyone else.

### Where It's At

Location may be a significant factor in college selection. Like the colleges themselves, locations vary in size from hamlets of a few hundred people to the largest cities in the country. The right school may be located anywhere from the Iowa cornfields to a New York City high-rise. Generally, it makes sense to factor the size, resources, and services of the college or university in with the size, resources, and services of the village, town, or city in which it's located. A number of huge universities are located in rural areas. Small cities unto themselves, they provide a relatively cosmopolitan atmosphere in the midst of rural isolation. Small colleges have a harder time compensating for rural or small town isolation. On the other hand, many students from these schools absolutely love the environment of a small college in a small town.

Colleges and universities in urban settings pose unique issues. Students need to be comfortable living relatively independently in a large city. As much as any school can provide an environment relatively oblivious to urban blight, the campuses cannot be totally immune, especially to safety threats, which vary, of course, with specific location. In any case, one reason for going to a city school is to take advantage of the location. Amidst a city with an abundance of cultural, intellectual, and recreational opportunities, students need to be prepared to negotiate modern, urban American life. It's not a death-defying challenge. Millions of students do it everyday! Students, their families, and guidance counselors simply should be aware of the varying demands and opportunities different locations provide.

A quick final thought on size and, especially, location: I hate to sound like someone's dad, but when you're eighteen, you don't know what you don't know. Eighteen-year-olds may not know what kind of environment they would be comfortable in. A city slicker who gets woozy at the sight of a cornfield might be totally transformed by rural charm. Perhaps not having to pass through a metal detector to go to class would seal the deal on the benefits of small town life. And what about the 4H champ for whom college in the big city is about as appealing as flat tires on her monster truck? Maybe it's time to try something new and get off the farm. This could be the opportunity of a lifetime.

In most cases, the educational experience far outweighs the impact of a school's physical location. Students should make informed choices about the size and location of the school they will attend, maybe for the very purpose of stepping outside their comfort zone. That may be the first step toward a great education.

### General Atmosphere

How do you get a sense of the general atmosphere of a college or university? What is the overall ambiance? Are people friendly and outgoing, or do they keep to themselves? Is the mood relaxed, or do students seem to barricade themselves in the library, coming up for air only to refill on double espresso so that they can study all night? Do the professors care about students as individuals, or are they seen as just cogs on the academic assembly line?

It's difficult, if not impossible, to gauge how a student will feel after settling into a new environment. In most cases, students, parents, and guidance counselors simply will not have enough data to make an informed decision about the environment prior to enrolling. When I was applying to college in 1970, I almost chose one school because on the Friday afternoon that I visited, Frisbees were flying through the air, long-haired students were hanging out in the quads listening to music, and at least one student gave me a "Hey, dude!" as my father and I walked past. (I think he was talking to me, not my father.) I wound up not going to that school and have no regrets — other than not having learned cool ways to toss a Frisbee.

The best way to get beneath the exterior trappings extolled by the admissions program of a college is to spend as much time as possible on its campus. As I recommend to students at the end of Chapter One, a DIY (Do-It-Yourself) visit may be the best way to judge the character of a place, especially if it is possible to spend a night or two, drop in on classes, and just hang out.

For many students with learning disabilities, it's important to attend a school where students are individuals rather than numbers. The idea of anonymity may be appealing after years of being singled out for being different or disabled, but with the exception of a few highly motivated, confident, and brave souls, the college experience works best when the student is connected, especially to other people, particularly service providers and professors.

As I've said, small colleges generally make personal contact more accessible, but many large universities certainly can provide a supportive environment if the student seeks it out. Even if the student, parents, and guidance counselor are satisfied with the type of support services provided, they should still try to dig a little deeper. What are the disability politics of the institution? Does support services have a friendly working relationship with faculty and administration, or is the relationship contentious and combative? I have observed programs where the dedication, resolve, and expertise of the disabilities staff were beyond question, yet they found themselves constantly fighting the rest of the institution. If receiving reasonable accommodations means fighting at every turn, you may wish to consider if this is the right environment, no matter how supportive and skillful the disability services staff may be. On the other hand, a school whose disability services staff, faculty, administration, and students are all on the same page is much more appealing. In this kind of environment, being a student with learning disabilities is no big deal. The institution as a whole works with the student and is more interested in seeing the student succeed than in arguing whether the whole "LD thing" is legitimate.

In addition to getting a sense of disability politics, it's equally useful to get a sense of the student body. Be careful not to make generalizations. Most campuses strive to create a diverse community; if a student does not like one group of people, a completely different group is waiting around the corner. A student who looks for compatible peers will find them. For most students, part of the college experience is branching out and opening up to all sorts of new possibilities, including new and different kinds of people. At the college where I teach, we ask incoming students to step outside their comfort zones. For many college students, social and personal growth over four years is as significant as intellectual development.

Students with learning disabilities have unique issues that other students don't face. Assuming that the student, parents, and guidance counselor are seeking a college or university with a good learning disabilities support program, it's useful to know what percentage of students have learning disabilities. A number of schools focus on meeting the needs of students with learning disabilities, the majority of whom have documented learning difficulties. The support that these schools offer is amazing. Not surprisingly, an important goal for these types of institutions is to assist students in developing self-understanding, self-advocacy, and the ability to use support services. In some cases, every student works with an advisor who is trained in helping students with learning disabilities develop these skills.

As a result, a number of institutions, whether by design or happenstance, are known as "LD colleges." Certainly an advantage of such a school is that almost everyone — teachers, administrators, and other students — understands what it means to have learning disabilities. A potential disadvantage is that many students with learning disabilities don't want to spend four years in a predominantly LD environment.

Some colleges that are not exclusively for students with learning disabilities have developed such comprehensive programs that they consistently attract large numbers of students with learning disabilities.

A sense of the identity of the institution and the individual's relationship to it is important for students with learning disabilities. At a conference in the mid 1990s, I was speaking to a representative of a college with a well established and prestigious learning disability support program, a place known as an LD college. I was complaining that my institution was not on board with our disability services program. We had implemented a comprehensive program of services and support for students with learning disabilities that apparently was garnering a word-of-mouth reputation. As a result, the number of students in the program had been growing. Some faculty members voiced displeasure at the idea that we were on the verge of becoming one of those LD colleges. What's so bad about that, I wondered? In my conversation with this representative, I dismissed the complaints of these faculty members rather brusquely. Much to my surprise, she said the professors had a point (although perhaps not exactly the one they intended to make).

Many college-bound students with learning disabilities are pretty tired of being identified as "special ed" students. They are tired of being labeled by the school system, of being singled out for what they have trouble doing rather than for what they are good at doing. They don't want to go to a college that reinforces this identity, where they will, in effect, wear their LD label rather publicly. Many college-bound students who have been successful academically, in spite of expectations to the contrary, want to attend traditional colleges, with the prestige that comes with studying at such institutions. They want to be more independent, to face new challenges. In fact, they may want to face the challenges of a world where learning disabilities are not the first concern, a world more like the real one they will face after graduation. They want to be like everyone else. In many ways, the school system may have denied them this basic right in elementary and high school. They've had to work to prove that they could be successful academically in spite of learning differently. They've earned the right to loosen their LD identity. "So don't become an LD college," my colleague told me. "You serve the needs of many students with learning disabilities more effectively by being a traditional college (with a good support program). You give them a choice."

As I said, it's hard to know what a school is really like until one is enrolled. Once at the school, a student may have different feelings about it each year. We've all seen alumni tearing up as they sing the alma mater after the big game. Their sense of the place has changed even more in retrospect; it's hard to imagine they carried on the same way when they were students.

My experience at college was not exactly what I had expected. There were times of confusion, frustration, anger, apathy, and occasional thoughts of going elsewhere — another school, home, a commune (remember how long ago I went to college). And this was during freshman orientation! But I learned that college meant adapting to new things. In retrospect, I found great satisfaction in dealing with the unexpected. College is, by design, a time of discovery. Discovery takes you out of your comfort zone. College isn't for someone who wants to stay in that zone.

## Tips for Students

### *It's Never too Early to get Serious About College*

What kind of college will you want to consider? Do you picture yourself strolling the campus of a traditional college or university? Perhaps it's one of those places with ivy-covered red brick buildings, tree-lined walkways, and initials carved on desks going back to the 1700s? Or maybe you see yourself at your state university, a small city populated almost exclusively by thousands of rowdy (and otherwise) kids? You need to make informed decisions about the kind of school you choose. You may wind up knowing more than your parents or guidance counselor.

You'll have to speak up for yourself if what you know is going to mean anything. If you're not in the center of this process, who is? Dude, you need to get in control. This is your life we're talking about here. Knowledge is power, but it doesn't do a lot of good if you don't do anything with it. You've got to make it happen. You need to stand up for yourself in a way that works for you, not against you. Getting in your parents' faces (or teachers' or counselors') is usually a recipe for arguments. There's nothing wrong with being likable while you look out for Number One. It's called having good social skills.

Once you're at college, a repertoire of self-advocacy skills will serve you well. Self-advocacy does not mean going it alone. It means using resources and getting help when and where you need it – without being helpless. It begins with knowing who you are.

### How to Learn More About Yourself

Do you really know who you are? If you're like most people, you'll be asking yourself that question throughout your life. We're constantly changing, and it's hard to pin down who we are at any one moment. But, if you're thinking about going to college, you need to know a few things about yourself. Let's start with some easy but essential questions to consider in deciding to which colleges you'll apply: First, what's your GPA? What types of classes have you been taking? Many colleges rate you on an adjusted GPA reflecting only college preparatory courses. Next, where do you stand with standardized tests? Have you ever taken the SAT or ACT? If so, what are your scores? If not, it usually makes sense to do a "trial run" of the SAT or ACT by the end of your junior year. You may start earlier by taking the PSAT in tenth grade.

The PSAT is a great way to practice for the SAT. I suggest that students with learning disabilities take a test preparation course. Doing well on the SAT, in particular, has a lot to do with knowing how to take the test. Kaplan, the Princeton Review, Peterson's, and even the College Board (the makers of the SAT) offer classroom-based courses, online help, and study guides. Google "SAT prep courses" to get an idea of how much help is available. If the SAT is a real concern, check out *Fairtest.org*. Many colleges and universities are de-emphasizing test scores, in many cases making the SAT optional. This site lists colleges and universities across the country that don't use SAT or ACT scores in the admissions process.

Other concerns besides grades and test scores may arise related to the specific nature of your learning disabilities. Professionals versed in an applied understanding of different kinds of learning styles and their effect on studying, learning, and performing can help you understand and address your specific disabilities. This process should begin with an assessment or discussion of your strengths, weaknesses, and needs.

A clear understanding of your disabilities will equip you to determine your needs and the strategies to meet them. For example, if you have difficulties with reading, you will need to consider what this may mean in terms of dealing with the demands of college. Can you work on ways of becoming a more effective reader? Should you be exploring compensations or bypass strategies such as books on tape? Do you need to expand your familiarity with literature so that you will have the kind of background that is expected of a college student?

Reading is only one example of a possible deficit area that should be addressed in pragmatic terms. You will need to look at all academic areas and start developing plans. In my experience, the areas of greatest concern for college students with learning disabilities (besides reading, writing, and math) are study skills, time management, and test-taking skills. It seems that many students entering college with and without learning disabilities simply don't know how to study, manage their time, or take tests strategically. You may actually enter college at an advantage over other students if you can tackle these issues while you're still in high school.

It's equally important to consider your strengths. Are you better in some subjects than in others? Do you have a particular aptitude for creative writing, math, music, art, computers, and so on? Are you a people person who works well in cooperative groups? This isn't the time for false modesty or for selling yourself short. You undoubtedly have talents. Don't worry if you don't see how your strengths can help you to be successful in college. There are countless ways for college students to meet with success. The important thing is to identify and acknowledge your strengths, whatever they may be.

Right now you're probably thinking, "This all sounds good, but how I do get the process started?" Remember all that stuff about your IEP team in the beginning of this book? Your IEP team should do more than just have meetings and talk about you. This is a time when you will want to ask your team for an updated evaluation and learning strategies assessment. Your team should help you discover how your unique abilities can lay the foundation for a successful college career. You might be able to jumpstart this whole process yourself, but in most cases, it probably makes sense to get mom or dad or your guidance counselor involved. Tell them you want to schedule a meeting of your IEP team to discuss getting ready for college.

### *What to Do When You Visit a College*

Talking with people about a college may provide important insights, but a visit will paint a more complete picture. In the field of learning disabilities, we talk a great deal about different styles of learning and how many individuals learn best experientially. Learning about college should be no exception.

Ideally, a visit should take place when school is in session. There are two ways to get this experience. One way is DIY (Do It Yourself), meaning you simply show up and start exploring. Many campuses have visitor or information centers. You may be able to take a guided tour; at a minimum, you'll find maps and brochures. If you're outgoing and comfortable talking to strangers, you might be able to chat with students, possibly even some professors and administrators. At larger institutions, you may be able to walk into a large lecture hall and attend a class.

The advantage of a DIY visit is that you see life as it is. The disadvantages are that you may not know what to look for, or if you do, it may not be accessible. It really helps to know someone at the school with whom you can stay for a day or two. Without a personal contact who can also give you the insider viewpoint, you will have to rely on the admissions program. Since it's their job to sell the school, the admissions office will show you the best face of the college, but to get beneath the surface you must take the initiative.

The other kind of visit is prearranged, usually through the admissions department. Many colleges have programs for prospective students that range from tours to weekend stays, usually in residence halls. As a student with learning disabilities, you will want to make a special point of checking out disability support services or the learning disabilities support program. Clearly, a prearranged visit will allow you to see and learn about the school in much greater detail than a DIY. At the same time, your experience is largely orchestrated. Also, many of these prospective student programs are limited to high school seniors who have completed and submitted their applications. Therefore, you are best to restrict this type of visit to a select few schools — the ones you are most likely to actually apply to in your senior year. In any case, time and logistics will limit the number of visits you can make. If possible, DIY visits can act as a screening process. In fact, some families devote a week or so during summer vacation to taking quick tours of several colleges. If you like what you see, you should schedule a second, formal visit in your senior year.

### Filling out Your Application

Filling out a college application can be a daunting process for both you and your parents. Attention to detail is very important. This isn't a situation where spelling and grammar don't count. Use whatever resources are available to help you generate a "clean copy." Of course, you will need to answer the essay question yourself, but you're entitled to whatever accommodations you've used in high school, from using spell-check on a computer to dictating to a scribe. The point here is to do the best job possible in representing yourself.

A major decision you must make at the time of applying is whether or not you will disclose that you have learning disabilities. Federal law is quite clear in protecting your right to make this decision. No one can force you to disclose; an application form requiring you to disclose or list any disability is violating your rights under the law. Consequently, you need to make an important legal decision even as you fill out application forms. Do you want the institution to know that you are a student with learning disabilities? You might be concerned that if the college knows that you have learning disabilities, it will not accept you. You can put your fears to rest. A school cannot decline to accept you because you have learning disabilities. To do so would be discrimination, and it's illegal. *As long as you meet the college's admissions requirements*, you are a qualified applicant, with or without learning disabilities.

From my experience, it makes sense in almost all cases to be upfront about your learning disabilities. I am not saying that colleges never discriminate against students with learning disabilities. The admissions process, particularly at academically competitive schools, can be pretty hazy as to what constitutes a "qualified" student. Seemingly qualified students are routinely rejected because the competition is so fierce. I have also heard stories that some admissions programs "smoke out" applicants with learning disabilities — even when they have not disclosed — by checking to see, for instance, if they had accommodations such as extended time on the SAT. But I believe these practices are few and far between. The vast majority of colleges and universities comply with disability rights laws and are extremely wary of winding up in court on disability discrimination charges.

There are several advantages to identifying yourself as a student with learning disabilities in the admissions process. Some students with learning disabilities have the aptitude and ability to succeed in the college or university of their choice but don't test well, particularly on admissions tests such as the SAT. Their scores might not make them competitive with other students. If admissions personnel are aware that SAT scores may be more reflective of a difficulty taking standardized tests than of the student's true ability, they might be more willing to look at the big picture. Another situation I have observed involves students who were not identified with learning disabilities until junior or senior year of high school. These students may have struggled academically in the first years of high school, largely because of a lack of support services. With accommodations and support in place, grades improve. Nevertheless, the college or university may base admissions decisions on the cumulative GPA from all four years. In this case, having a context in which to consider lower grades and subsequent improvement may significantly help your chances of being admitted.

You may or may not wish to talk about your learning disabilities in your admissions essay question. I have read a number of impressive essays where the applicant discusses the effects of having learning disabilities. Generally, this type of essay demonstrates a significant degree of insight and self-understanding. In some cases, it's clear that the applicant has "reframed" the learning disabilities experience, demonstrating a recognition of learning style and differences, an acceptance of who he or she is, an understanding of strengths and weaknesses, and a sense or plan of how to deal with life. These essays tend to be inspiring. They help the reader appreciate the struggle of coping with learning disabilities. At the same time, they focus on the positive, particularly how the student has been able to cope, compensate, and overcome. Such an essay tells the admissions counselor that you're ready for college. You know that you will have challenges, but you've already thought about how to meet them. You're showing that you're serious about college, and you would not be at this point if you had not worked hard at your education. If you're stuck, ask a friend, parent, guidance counselor, or even an admissions counselor for help.

On the other hand, some students write essays about their learning disabilities that sound like excuses or "poor me" pleas. Trying to make an admissions counselor feel sorry for you isn't likely to open any doors. Blame, anger, confusion, and self-pity are not good selling points. More importantly, if this is how you really see yourself and the world around you, you may not be ready for college. You will be expected to take care of yourself, to be accountable, to be tough. If you're planning to go to college, make sure that you really want to take on this challenge. Don't apply to college because you're "supposed to," because your friends are doing it, because your parents have been wanting this all your life. Do it because you want to, because you're ready to take on challenges that may be harder than any you have faced so far.

As part of the overall application process, creating a resume may be beneficial. Most applications to colleges and universities don't require resumes, but a resume can be an impressive addition to the application packet. Additionally, creating a resume will help you organize important information about yourself into one place. You may find this to be a helpful resource in answering specific application questions as well as providing material for essay questions. If you don't have an interview, the essay is the only chance for admissions to get to know you. So take great care — you only get one chance to make a first impression.

---

**Exhibit 1.5. Tips for Writing the Admissions Essay**

### _DO_

- Tell your own story.
- Use your own voice.
- Ask your best friend, "What's the best story I've told you about myself?"
- Be unique. Remember admissions officers have to read thousands of essays.
- Consider length. An essay that's short looks like you don't care. One that's too long loses the reader's interest.
- Follow guidelines.
- Allow enough time to share your essay with at least one or more persons who will proofread and offer commentary/suggestions.

### _DON'T_

- Ask or allow a parent or tutor to write your essay.
- Procrastinate.
- Just write what you think they want to hear.
- Think too much.
- Compare yourself to an ideal applicant.
- Send a first draft.
- Rely on spell check alone. Admissions counselors circle spelling and grammar mistakes.
- Use humor if you've never used it before — the application essay is not the place to start.

---

### *Friendly Advice from a Dean of Admissions*

(special thanks to Martha O'Connell, Dean of Admissions, McDaniel College)

• Ask yourself, "Why am I going to college?"

• Knowing yourself is the first step to finding the right fit.

• First impressions matter, starting with your first phone call or email.

• Put together a nice looking application. White Out does not win points with admissions counselors.

• Don't leave campus right after your interview. Take a tour of the school. Look at how students dress — if you're put off by preppies, take note of the amount of Lacoste, L.L. Bean, or J. Crew.

• Colleges want to be loved, too. Show an interest during the interview and tour. Let them know that they're your favorite (even if they're not).

• Don't go overboard. Flattery can get you busted. Admissions counselors have good crap detectors... in other words, don't be insincere!

• Talk about what interests you most, but don't pull out a laundry list of activities.

• You have something unique to offer. Colleges are not looking for everyone to be the same.

• Extracurricular activities don't just take place at school. Engaging in activities at home, having a job, or being involved in your community demonstrates time management skills.

• Admissions counselors have active imaginations. If something needs to be explained, explain it, but don't make excuses.

- Know and understand your test scores and grades.
- Don't take the SAT more than twice.
- Limit applications to four or five colleges or universities.
- When you set up a visit, know what to expect. You may or may not be able to attend a class, talk to students, etc.
- Get the inside 411. Call an admissions office and ask whatever you need to ask. If you're worried about being tagged, use a fake name.

## Tips for Parents

### *If You Enable, Your Child May Be Unable*

How can you help your child with learning disabilities get into college and be successful? Perhaps the process really begins with you, the parents. Do you want your child to go to college? Most importantly, does your child want to go to college? It's true that college isn't for everyone. At the same time, don't underestimate the potential of students with learning disabilities to make it in college. I've spoken with many successful adults with learning disabilities who graduated from college. Many of them earned graduate degrees as well. You would be amazed at how many of them were told that they would never make it in college — that they were not college material. And many of these comments came from high school guidance counselors. A guidance counselor once told a high school student with learning disabilities that he was a "J.I.T." — a janitor-in-training.

Luckily, this individual ignored those comments, was successful in college, and now makes a hefty six-figure salary as an executive in a major corporation. Some janitor!

Parents have an important role in helping their college-bound children with learning disabilities develop and use self-advocacy skills. I recommend starting to think about college as early as eighth or ninth grade. Most eighth and ninth graders are hardly ready to be planning for college. They're way too busy with video games, sports, staying connected, looking cool, and thinking their parents are about the dumbest losers on the planet. Believe me, at this age kids need a lot of support (or a good kick) – as long as they don't think you're actually involved.

The initial planning for college falls to most parents, but the ultimate goal is for your child to be a self-advocate who is as independent, autonomous, and self-directed a young adult as possible. Keep reminding yourself of this, and learn how to back off – gracefully, gently, and effectively. Many parents of students with learning disabilities have had to fight hard and be advocates for their children through elementary, middle, and high school. Often, they take on the same role in college, much to the detriment of their child. One of the biggest complaints from staff in our program for students with learning disabilities is the intrusiveness of some parents. It's as if the parent is the one going to school, not the child. Moreover, many of these parents have a sense of entitlement because they're the ones taking out loans to pay for college. The attitude is understandable, but it usually results in a reputation of being a nuisance. Service providers are professionals who have chosen to support college students with learning disabilities; they are not thrilled at being second-guessed or accused of not doing enough.

Parents have less of a tendency to be overly involved in their college student's life if they are able to let go — or at least make a conscious effort to help their child acquire and use self-advocacy skills. *You* will probably have to start the conversations about college. *You* will probably have to request the first IEP/transition planning meeting. *You* may have to be insistent and persistent. But *you* can also hand over much of the responsibility to your child throughout high school.

Empowering younger adolescents begins with active listening skills. It's not enough merely to listen; you have to know how to draw out thoughtful dialogue from your child. Don't expect your eighth, ninth, or even tenth grader to take a lot of initiative. In the beginning stages of simply thinking about college, you should maximize your child's involvement. As obvious as it sounds, this is about your child, not about you, even though you know what is best (just like your parents did)! Your input is valuable and necessary, but it takes a secondary role to your child's own active involvement. Come to think of it, why isn't self-advocacy an access skill on the IEP form? When the whole team helps the student to learn and use self-advocacy skills, both within the IEP meeting and beyond, the student is given the opportunity to get involved, take some initiative, and gain control. The following section provides some suggestions for empowering college-bound students.

## The IEP — Where Do You Fit In? Where Do You Stay Out?

An adult friend with learning disabilities remembers that his parents were very involved in the IEP process. They developed and monitored their son's goals and objectives and made sure that he received a quality education. He said his IEP was really a PEP (Parents' Education Program) because it had more to do with what his parents wanted and expected than with his own goals. He even had some difficulty with his college's disability services. Because the goals set by his parents were not truly his, he was not interested in them and was unwilling to utilize recommendations or accommodations. As he began to develop his own goals, he had to undergo additional testing with disability services because his goals were not the ones that had been officially documented. If you're making the decisions about the courses your child should take in twelfth grade, you may be on the verge of continuing a relationship of codependency into college and beyond.

Please understand, I am not suggesting abandoning your child the moment she or he turns eighteen. As you will see in Chapter Two of this book, you may continue to be an effective (and empowering) support system for your child during college and even beyond. As opposed to many members of my generation who wanted out of the nuclear family as soon as possible (at least until the macrobiotic diet and hard work of the commune drove us back home), many children today see their parents as partners and supporters who are resources for information and guides for sound decision making. I could not have imagined my parents sitting in on an appointment with a dean or professor when I was in college in the early 1970s. Maybe I was missing something. Many of my most productive meetings with students occur when parents attend, at least those parents who balance their concerns with respect for their young adult's independence and autonomy.

Even if you encourage and support your child in building self-advocacy and independence skills, your child may opt to put on the brakes. As much as educators complain about "helicopter parents" (always hovering around their child), sometimes it's the kids who don't want to let go. I've had students in my office ask me to call their parents to get their opinion. Our director of campus safety told me that when a campus safety officer was in the process of writing up a student for some sort of infraction, the student pulled out her cell phone and told the officer, "Talk to my father." It's hard to imagine that the parents in these cases had not contributed to their children's dependence. You can smugly say, "I'm not like that," but I think it's hard *not* to be an overly protective, overly involved parent today. Whether it's good or whether it's bad, social, cultural, political, and economic factors increasingly define this style as the norm. Those forces are difficult to resist.

So, what can parents do? Has the zeitgeist of the twenty-first century sentenced parents and children to life-long co-dependency? Although it's not entirely bad for many high school and college kids to have much closer relationships with their parents than I did at that age, at the same time, parents must recognize the critical importance of letting their chicks fly — of kicking them out of the nest if necessary. Just as children have to make transitions to get ready for college, parents have to transition to being more like partners and less like dictators.

Similarly, the parent role in IEP meetings should change over time. At first, you may be the one making the meeting happen, checking in with school officials, advocating for your child through a working understanding of IDEA 2004 and the ADA. You're probably the one who's getting your kid involved. You might have to be a therapist just to get your kid to even talk about college, and you undoubtedly will counsel her or him throughout the entire process. Although you may be doing all of these things, you still need to encourage your child to be more independent. You need to help your child acquire and use self-advocacy skills.

By twelfth grade, your child should have a lead role in the IEP meeting. Questions about the student should be directed to the student. Responses should be from the student. This does not mean that your child is the unchallenged authority on all IEP matters. In fact, constructive disagreement is part of the adult world. However, it generally makes more sense for family members to be on the same page before the meeting. Advance family discussion also helps students and their parents prepare questions, identify issues, define roles, and even practice self-advocacy skills.

---

**Exhibit 1.6. Tips for Parents at IEP Meetings**

### *DO*

- Initiate transition planning starting in ninth grade.
- Request the college guidance counselor attend IEP meetings related to transition planning.
- Ask for an overview of the college prep curriculum.
- Explore options for supporting academic success, including tutoring and summer classes.
- Demand a psychoeducational evaluation in eleventh or twelfth grade.
- Review recent documentation.
- Make sure appropriate accommodations, recommendations, and academic adjustments for college are explicitly stated in updated documentation.
- Request the IEP team sign off on appropriate accommodations, recommendations, and academic adjustments for college in updated documentation.
- Encourage your child to become more involved with these tasks over the course of high school.

### *DON'T*

- Come to an IEP meeting without your child.
- Speak for your child.
- Take "no" for an answer without exploring your rights
- Expect the IEP team to do all the work.
- Assume you know what works for your child without checking.

---

## *Cost, or How Will We Ever Pay for This?*

Cost clearly may be the make or break issue in choosing a college or university. No matter how you slice it, a college education is expensive, ranging from possibly less than $1,000 for full-time tuition at a local, non-residential community college, to total fees in excess of $40,000 per year at some private institutions. By the time you read this, costs will probably be even higher.

For a small minority of families, cost may not be an issue, but in almost all cases, financing a college education means trying to find some financial help. Your family needs to consider how to meet the costs of your child's college education. Financial aid takes two forms: loans and a reduction in fees. It's great if fees are low enough to pay outright, but most families find that they also need loans to help them cope with the expenses. A college education costs a great deal of money upfront and often results in long-term debt. You need to make sure your child is serious about attending college before taking on this type of commitment.

Oftentimes, parents only allow their child to apply to colleges that they believe they can afford; but don't be so quick to rule out higher-priced schools. The money game isn't exactly what it seems — and it is somewhat of a game. Virtually all colleges and universities offer some type of need-based financial assistance. In this case, the more money you have, the less financial aid your child will receive; the less money you have, the aid more you get; and the more expensive the college, the more money you get. Although it may sound too good to be true, colleges with sticker-shock tuitions and fees realize that few students and their families can really afford such costs. In many ways, college fees work on a kind of sliding scale. Based on your financial worth, the college's financial aid department determines what they believe you can afford. In many cases, the difference is made up through loans and work-study. This aspect of paying for college begins to put a measure of responsibility on your child, who usually becomes responsible for the loan. With having to work to get through college as part of the package, your child, like it or not, is invested in her or his education.

You'll probably want to look into outside resources for

financial support. From running up your credit card to taking out a second mortgage or a home equity loan, financing your child's education is challenging. Certain loans offer tax advantages, and may be preferable (or at least complementary) to a student loan.

Loans, of course, are not the only way to finance a college education. Depending on their assessment of your financial need and ability, many institutions will offer a lower tuition. You simply pay less and also get a loan to make up the difference. A select few institutions are doing away with loans altogether. Instead, they lower their fees to try to make tuition affordable for you. You will not need a loan to make up the difference, because there should be no difference in what you are able to pay and the cost of tuition. While this approach is rare at present, it may signal a trend making education available to anyone who qualifies. Of course, "qualifying" is a serious issue. Highly selective schools that offer strong financial aid packages become even more attractive and consequently, even more selective. Financial aid is readily available, and the best packages get the most competition.

Competition is a traditional way of securing financial assistance in the form of scholarships. The majority of scholarships are academic, usually connected to grade point average. Athletic scholarships are also available, but in spite of all the attention given to student-athletes, only a very small percentage of high school athletes ever receive a free ride. If an athletic scholarship is a possibility, you will undoubtedly know about it. Coaches will be calling your child at all hours. If they aren't coming to you, don't put much hope in receiving this kind of assistance.

Students with learning disabilities may feel at a disadvantage in obtaining academic scholarships. Your child has probably struggled with school; good grades have not come easily. SAT scores of students with learning disabilities are generally lower than those of students without learning disabilities. You might think that scholarships are only for the very top students, and naturally, top students do tend to have the best shot at getting them. But you would be surprised at the range of scholarship opportunities available.

The Internet has revolutionized scholarship hunting. Begin your search by visiting the websites www.collegeanswer.com or www.fastweb.com. At this point, your child needs to assume responsibility for the process. To use these web services, students need to register and provide information about themselves. It makes sense to register on such sites starting in spring of junior year.

Use technology, but don't overlook sources for scholarships that may be in your own backyard. Local civic organizations such as the Lions, Rotary, and Kiwanis clubs often provide college scholarships for local high school students. Businesses, agencies, clubs, corporations, institutions, and foundations, large and small, national and local, may provide scholarship money, ranging from a couple-hundred dollars to full tuition, room and board. Ask your child's high school guidance counselor for information about local funding and other possibilities.

There are a few scholarships specifically for college-bound students with learning disabilities (LD Online has some helpful resources at http://www.ldonline.org/ ld_indepth/transition/college_financial_aid.html). Most colleges and universities also have their own scholarship packages. The criteria for awarding scholarships vary widely. Scholarships exist for students who are very involved in extracurricular activities, who demonstrate leadership qualities, or who demonstrate strong character. Don't assume that your child cannot earn a scholarship. Check out every available resource. Most institutions offer their own scholarships, but before your child even begins to apply to college, you should look into other sources.

### *Filling out Financial Aid Forms*

To apply for almost any kind of financial aid, you will need to fill out the Free Application for Federal Student Aid (FAFSA) form. You may fill it out online at www.fafsa.ed.gov or pick up hardcopy at many libraries and college financial aid offices. Begin this process no later than January of your child's senior year. Some institutions have deadlines as early January 15 for need-based aid. You will need your tax returns from the year before, pay stubs, and a preliminary tax return. Obviously, information about last year's income to compute a tax return may not be available in early January. Check a box on the form that asks you to make a best estimate, which you will update after filing your tax return. You will need to provide some additional information: untaxed income, money that you put into retirement last year (but not your actual retirement account), asset information including real estate but excluding home and retirement. Assets don't carry that much weight; your income will largely determine the aid you receive. FAFSA allows you to send out applications to six schools or state agencies.

Colleges and universities that have their own financial aid programs will require more forms. Fill these out as early as possible, usually by March. Most institutions like to offer the award with the acceptance letter. Institutional financial aid forms will often dig deeper, asking about home equity, tuition expenses for other children in college, who does and who doesn't live in the household, outside scholarships, non-custodial parent information, and possibly a profile. The College Board has an excellent website that allows you to establish a free, online profile, as well as extensive information about testing, planning, applying, and paying for college at http://www.collegeboard.com/splash.

---

**Exhibit 1.7. Tips for Financial Aid**

### <u>*DO*</u>

- Maintain well-ordered and comprehensive financial records dating back at least two years.
- Be relentless.
- Use the web to maximum advantage (but keep your credit card in your wallet).
- Be consistent with the information you provide for FAFSA and the college's financial aid office.
- Check out http://www.collegeboard.com/splash to jump-start the whole process.
- Follow **ALL** directions on forms.
- Complete **EVERY** item on forms. Missing = tossed.

### <u>*DON'T*</u>

- Assume you can't get financial aid.
- Pay a fee to websites to help with FAFSA or other financial aid forms.
- Miss deadlines.
- Try to alter your financial picture (sometimes known as a felony!).

---

# Tips for Guidance Counselors

*Promoting Self-Awareness and Self-Advocacy*

As a guidance counselor, one of the best things you can do for college-bound students with learning disabilities is to help them develop self-determination and self-reliance. You are preparing your students for an educational environment where they will be largely responsible for their educational support systems. They need to learn self-advocacy skills in high school in order to be successful in college. Self-advocacy skills must be grounded in self-understanding. That is, in order to advocate effectively for reasonable accommodations, the student must understand what works, what does not work, what works in some places but not in others, and what doesn't work at all. To the extent that you have the time, you can play a major role in helping your students make the transition to college life.

If approached creatively, the IEP meeting can be the straw that stirs the drink. The IEP presents the best opportunity to review documentation and make a variety of observations. By asking the right questions, you can use the meeting as a forum to discuss learning style, strengths, weaknesses, study suggestions/strategies, and accommodations (why they may be helpful). The meeting gives you and the student an opportunity to gain understanding and insight, the foundations of successful self-advocacy.

## *Your Role in the IEP*

IDEA 2004 mandates transition planning for all students fourteen and older with IEPs. However, the guidelines for transition planning are vague. If you are working with a student with learning disabilities who is considering college, contact the student's IEP coordinator to set up meetings specifically devoted to college transition planning. The IEP team should determine what kinds of services the student will need in order to make a successful transition to college. For some students, little transition planning is needed. As we know, some students with learning disabilities excel academically in high school. They have high GPAs and high SAT scores, and have had little need for special education services. Such students can apply to colleges of their choice without worrying about whether these colleges have good support programs for students with learning disabilities. More typically, however, you will need to work with the team and the student to develop a transition plan.

The IEP team assists students in deciding what type of postsecondary option makes the most sense for them. You may want to have your student look at career and interest inventories. Equally important, the student's skills, knowledge, competencies, and educational preparation should be assessed. Based on educational background, aptitude, and achievement thus far, you and the IEP team can make a realistic determination about where the student might be headed. During the time the student is considering college, the transition planning part of the IEP should focus on self-awareness and self-advocacy.

---

**Exhibit 1.8. Five Questions Guidance Counselors Should Ask at IEP Meetings**

1. Learning style — How do we describe the learning style of the student?
2. Strengths — What are the student's strengths (academic, extracurricular, social, etc.)?
3. Weaknesses — What are the student's weaknesses (academic, extracurricular, social, etc.)?
4. Strategies — What kinds of strategies (study skills, compensations, bypass strategies, etc.) help this student in different subjects?
5. Accommodations — What kind of accommodations will be important in college?

---

### *Course Selection in High School*

Traditionally, college-bound students take two years of algebra, a year of geometry, two years of foreign language, American history, lab science, literature and writing courses, and ideally some honors-level courses. Will extra preparation be in order to help the student handle these various courses? Are summer classes a viable option? Will some courses need to be waived? If so, colleges that have more liberal entrance standards and permit waivers for some requirements should be on the top of your college prospect list. Colleges and universities are becoming much more accommodating in evaluating and working with students with learning disabilities. For example, the National Collegiate Athletic Association (NCAA) has agreed to count some special education coursework toward requirements for athletic scholarships for students with learning disabilities. Nevertheless, I believe that a student with learning disabilities who plans to go to college, especially a competitive one, will want to complete as many traditional college prep courses as possible. The more the high school academic

51

experience matches the traditional college preparatory track, the easier the transition to postsecondary education. By ninth grade, a dedicated student with learning disabilities might need to consider additional preparation such as tutoring or summer courses in order to build skills needed to be successful in college preparatory courses.

### Kinds of Academic Programs Offered: An Unabashed Endorsement

Certain postsecondary education choices may place students on a particular career path; that is, technical institutes, business colleges, art schools, and so on prepare students for fairly specific careers. For some high school students who have a particular passion and know what they're good at and what they want to do, taking the direct route makes the most sense. A number of graduating high school seniors already know where they'd like to head in their education and career. For students who know they want to be doctors, declaring a pre-med program from the get-go isn't only appropriate, but practically necessary in order to meet all of the course requirements. However, most students with learning disabilities are not sure what career they want to persue. That is why I believe that liberal arts institutions or universities with significant humanities or general studies programs are the best choice for most students.

This book is geared toward "traditional" college-bound students with learning disabilities headed to schools that offer a "traditional" academic undergraduate education. Almost all of these institutions will expose students to various components of liberal arts, humanities, or general education. I am the product of a liberal arts college experience and teach at a liberal arts college. I am biased on this issue, so I present the following thoughts as personal and subjective (and hopefully persuasive):

A real tragedy occurs when an undecided student feels forced to make a definitive, but actually arbitrary choice of a particular program or concentration of study. In most schools, the vast majority of pre-med freshmen never make it to medical school. While we all need to take risks, some of those freshmen did not make good decisions in choosing a pre-med program. Many of these students regroup and proceed to find a course of study that suits them, but many labor for up to four years only to come up short and without a diploma. In fact, with the overall graduation rate of American colleges and universities estimated at less than 40% for four years and about 60% for six years, students only have about a 50/50 chance of even graduating. Choosing the right academic program may play a critical role in determining whether or not a student graduates.

For students who are not sure about what they want to do, liberal arts, humanities, or general education programs offer a great deal of variety and may help identify interests, strengths and weaknesses. Many students with learning disabilities have had difficulty with the rather narrow curriculum of high school. Even in college, they will have to wade into and through some required core courses in a liberal arts curriculum that often expose their areas of weakness. At the same time, a liberal arts curriculum will offer virtually unlimited opportunities to explore interests and strengths. Try to determine if your student has a passion for one of the traditional areas of education in the humanities and sciences, subjects such as history, literature, social sciences, life and physical sciences, to name a few.

If you recommend a liberal arts education to a student, you need to explain that this type of education isn't necessarily intended to get that student on a specific career track. It's not as if liberally educated students don't develop specific skills, but a liberal arts education isn't the mark of a technically trained professional.

Interestingly, many people in the business and professional world state that they prefer hiring new employees who have a liberal arts background. They recognize that completing an education grounded in critical thinking, writing, problem-solving, and logical decision making is a great foundation for all sorts of professions. Most liberal arts institutions claim that their graduates know how to problem solve, make good decisions, and communicate effectively. Instead of an emphasis on merely acquiring knowledge, a liberal arts education asks students to take that knowledge and analyze it, evaluate it, and arrive at logical, thoughtful conclusions. Certainly, any profession should find an individual with this background attractive. While a liberal arts degree alone may not guarantee a record-setting run on *Jeopardy* (although *Jeopardy* champ Ken Jennings has a B.A. in English literature), it does signify a meaningful and still prestigious set of skills and abilities.

Students with learning disabilities often find experiential learning to be their preferred mode. Many traditional liberal arts schools have come to share the philosophy that experiential, hands-on learning is a vital component of education. They've also learned that their students want and need some specific career training, or at least experience with a type of career. As a result, internships, service learning, and other kinds of direct experiences may be found at virtually all liberal arts institutions. Your students may want to include the availability of these kinds of experiences as criteria for making decisions about where to apply.

The reality of education and training in the beginning of the twenty-first century is that graduate or professional studies are often vital for successfully pursuing a career path; therefore, many graduates from liberal arts institutions or humanities and general education programs go on to graduate school. A number of highly successful adults with learning disabilities have told me that graduate school was the easiest and most meaningful part of their education. They were able to have educational experiences devoted solely to their areas of strength and interest.

A liberal arts education is intended to open students' minds to the endless possibilities of learning and self-growth, leaving them with a desire to further their education. Think about yourself in your role as guidance counselor. As you learn more about something (like understanding teenagers!), you tend to realize you have just scratched the surface. There is so much more to learn. I remember teachers telling me that by the end of college, I would discover that I knew less than I thought I did when I began. Talk about not knowing what you don't know! Instead of seeing the world as nicely, simply, and artificially divided into black and white, I have been forever moving back and forth between endless shades of gray.

Here's the secret lying beneath the liberal arts mystique: it's not for everyone. A liberal arts education may be the one opportunity in life to enjoy four years, give or take, of intellectual self-indulgence. Clichéd as it may be, a liberal arts education is about learning for learning's sake, a chance to pursue intellectual interests purely for the satisfaction of discovery. It's an education that profits from and cultivates a passion for learning. Not everyone has the luxury to devote four, often expensive, years to self-indulgence.

Perhaps you're beginning to think that only students who read Plato in the original Greek, stay up all night debating Nietzsche, and relax by factoring differential equations while listening to Verdi will do well in a liberal arts setting - don't sell your students short! One of my greatest joys is working with students who did not have a clue about what a liberal arts education meant when they first started college, but four years later the same students emerged profoundly and positively transformed. In the beginning, students may question the worth of taking courses or majoring in a subject that doesn't seem practical. "What kind of job am I going to get with a degree in history?" I've met with many students who think the only worthwhile degree is business. Their parents are often a driving force behind this outlook. At my college, we really believe in our motto, "We change lives." As students settle into a diet of learning for learning's sake, they do begin to change, and sometimes change profoundly. They do begin to grasp some of the Big Truths.

The Big Truth that I walked away from college with was the lasting value of my education. Virtually everything else in life is transient; we can lose our possessions, our health, our relationships — anything that we hold dear — in the blink of an eye. But no one can take our education away from us. For me, education has allowed me to see the world in a very different way. Once you open a student's mind to the limitless possibilities of the human intellect, no one can close it.

Do students really need to go to liberal arts schools to open their minds? Wouldn't it be easier and cheaper to do it by themselves? When I was taking my senior seminar in English literature, we asked the professor why our department was so old and stodgy and hung up on the classics. Why didn't the department offer courses in contemporary literature? He replied that it was presumed that, as well-educated people, we would read contemporary literature on our own, probably to be entertained rather than challenged; but he was pretty sure that most of us would not be picking up Chaucer, Milton, or Pope on our own. (I think they did allow that we might occasionally return to Shakespeare.) Surely, he reasoned, we did not want to miss the opportunity to read the great writers. The structure and the discipline of being in college was necessary to get us to challenge ourselves intellectually. Tests and papers were not designed merely to keep us busy and keep our parents happy; they were the necessary incentives (or evils) that, with the benefit of 20/20 hindsight, turned out to be part of the gift of our education. His simple response altered my thinking and lives within me on a daily basis. I am grateful for my liberal arts undergraduate education. It changed my life.

## CHAPTER TWO
## STAYING THERE: Self-Advocacy in College

# Three Things To Know

## What the Law Does and Does Not Provide

Going to college represents a major step toward independence. Up until now, the student may not have worried too much about self-advocacy because the system largely took care of ensuring services were provided. K-12 school law mandates that any student identified as having learning disabilities is entitled to special services. IDEA 2004 (discussed in Chapter One) guarantees that a student with learning disabilities will have an IEP and all that comes with it.

An extensive knowledge of their rights under the law is probably not all that critical for high school students with officially identified learning disabilities. For the most part, services are taken care of for the student. The IEP team meets on a regular basis, and the student, parent, and guidance counselor may participate in the meetings as well. A case manager, usually a special education teacher, makes sure that services and accommodations are in place. The one area that may require advocacy is transition planning, as discussed in Chapter One of this book.

Having evaluations and other pertinent material on file is the necessary first step towards getting accommodations, modifications, academic adjustments, and support services in college. The student must provide documentation of learning disabilities. The college or university will not provide any accommodation until the student goes to disability support services, provides a copy of a psychoeducational evaluation and/or a copy of the IEP, and requests services. As I mentioned in Chapter One, many colleges require that testing be current, that is, no more than three years old. Increasingly, colleges and universities are requiring comprehensive documentation with specific types of testing. The type of documentation will vary from institution to institution. Consequently, before entering a college or university, students, along with their parents and guidance counselors, will need to know the specific institutional requirements for documenting learning disabilities and other learning difficulties.

Under IDEA 2004, two groups of students may get left behind in elementary and high school: those with undiagnosed learning disabilities, and those with Attention Deficit Disorder (ADD). Learning disabilities are identified according to the specific guidelines of the special education laws of each state. A student who has learning problems but does not meet specific criteria for identification (the discrepancy formula that was discussed in the previous section), is out of luck in many cases. A diagnosis of Attention Deficit Disorder (with or without Hyperactivity) does not lead to an IEP or special services. A student with ADD might qualify for limited support with a "504" plan (this refers to Section 504 of the Rehabilitation Act of 1973), but only if someone such as a parent, teacher, or counselor pushes the system a little. Surprisingly, college may be a more welcoming environment for these students, provided they can obtain documentation that shows that their learning style poses a significant obstacle for success in college.

Without proper documentation provided expressly by the student, a college student isn't legally eligible for disability support services. By the end of senior year in high school, the student and parent should obtain all records, most importantly evaluation reports and IEPs. The family has a right to these records. Make multiple copies of them. Keep the originals in a safe yet easily accessible place. The moment students with learning disabilities leave high school, they are responsible for keeping track of all their records. For students with learning disabilities, or any disabilities for that matter, a significant sign of independence is a change in the ownership of and responsibility for documentation.

A student might not automatically start receiving services and assistance once the office of disability services has received appropriate documentation. Unlike IDEA 2004, the ADA does not require colleges and universities to offer special education services per se. Instead, schools must make sure that all educational programs and activities are available to students with disabilities, usually by providing reasonable accommodations or academic adjustments.

In the cases of persons with physical or sensory disabilities, the accommodations needed are usually obvious and don't require judgment calls. Most students who are severely hearing impaired need interpreters in classrooms in order to have the same opportunities as hearing students. A person who is blind may need books on tape or in Braille, and other assistance in dealing with visual and print material. A student in a wheelchair must be able to get into the building and classroom. Rarely does debate ensue anymore about providing such accommodations, adjustments, or services.

When it comes to being fair with (or not discriminating against) students with learning disabilities, the issues are not so clear. Colleges and universities have tremendous latitude in determining the "reasonableness" of accommodations or academic adjustments. The IEP and evaluation reports are powerful documents that should outline the types of services and support the student needs. Nevertheless, in many ways the student with learning disabilities starts all over again at the beginning of college. The college has the right to review documentation and then make its own decisions on what accommodations or specific services it will provide, sometimes not accepting accommodations that had been in place in high school.

Colleges and universities do have to demonstrate that such decisions provide students with learning disabilities equal access to the regular academic program. These determinations, usually made by the office of disability services, most often follow the recommendations and guidelines set forth in evaluations and IEPs; however, different institutions have different policies and practices. They may not be willing to implement what the IEP recommends or do what the student, parent(s), and/or guidance counselor thinks they should. A number of cases have made it clear that the courts don't want to micromanage how colleges and universities work with students with learning disabilities. Quite frankly, as long as they are using a systematic and consistent process in determining accommodations and services, the schools tend to have the upper hand.

What does this mean? For one, if a college has a policy that does not permit substitutions, waivers, or even accommodations for requirements such as foreign language or math, don't expect that it will make an exception. My college has a math proficiency requirement that states that all students must pass a basic skills (arithmetic computation) test and an algebra test. Calculators are not allowed on the basic skills test. I don't personally agree with this approach, but that, in fact, is irrelevant. We try to make this policy clear to prospective students. Yet, students with learning disabilities or their parents frequently besiege me, saying, "How can this be? We've got to have a calculator. We can't do computations without one. This is unfair. It must be illegal." However, the math department contends that the ability to compute is the essential skill being tested. I've checked with one of the foremost disability lawyers in the country, and guess what? The college has the right to determine what it considers to be the essentials of its curriculum.

## How to Use Disability Services

Almost all students with learning disabilities that I have known have benefited from a relationship with disability services (DS), particularly in their first year or two of college. For most students with learning disabilities, getting to know DS as early as possible is the most sensible approach. If the student disclosed learning disabilities in the admissions process, disability services may initiate contact. Students, parents, and guidance counselors can learn about support services through the college or university's website and through other college publications such as the catalog or material provided directly by disability services.

The names of support programs vary from college to college. The most common designation is Office of Disability Services (or Disability Support Services), often shortened to disability services or simply DS (the term I use in this book). Other places may call it the 504 Office or 504 Services (after Section 504). It could be known as the Learning Support Program, possibly even Services for Students with Learning Disabilities. Although most institutions have a program to work with students with any kind of disability, specialized programs for students with learning disabilities tend to be subsets of those programs. Some institutions, particularly small colleges, may have programs whose names are designed to hide or downplay the term, disability. Other institutions work with students with disabilities within academic support services available to all students, with and without disabilities. And some schools, more likely small ones, may not have a program, but rather an individual who provides assistance to students with learning disabilities. Admissions offices almost always have accurate information at the ready; Student Affairs or Activities, academic deans, advisors, and a number of other people on campus should be able to solve the mystery of finding support services.

In an initial meeting, an astute staff member will want to get to know the student. In many cases, the staff member will conduct some sort of intake assessment or interview. A good professional will begin to build rapport and try to put the student at ease. The student should use this time to get to know the staff member and to learn more about the program. Referencing the questions in Exhibit 2.1 is a good place for students to begin.

---

**Exhibit 2.1. Student Questions for Initial Meeting with DS**

• What is the background and training of this staff member and other staff?
• Will a case manager be assigned?
• What kinds of services are offered — tutoring, study and college survival skills, assistance with writing papers, counseling, help with course registration, etc.?
• Will regularly scheduled, one-on-one appointments take place?
• What assistive technology is available?

---

Each initial meeting with a DS staff member should be unique and individualized. DS staff and the student should discuss class schedule, types of courses, syllabi, and books as early as possible. Accommodations and support may (or may not) be different for each class. For example, a course in which the instructor posts complete lecture notes online probably does not require a notetaker. Extended time or a separate location for taking tests isn't necessary if only take-home tests are given.

These initial meetings are also the time to review documentation. Different DS programs have different ways of determining and setting up accommodations, adjustments, and specific services. In general, the process begins by looking at the documentation the student provides. The majority of programs will tend to implement the recommendations in the evaluation reports and/or the IEPs. As discussed in the previous section, colleges and universities are not required to provide special or individualized education programs, which means that they don't have to follow *all* the recommendations, particularly if these are more involved than the services the program typically offers. Nevertheless, most programs do provide accommodations such as extended time (usually 1.5 to 2 times, not unlimited) for tests and exams, separate locations for tests and exams, readers, books on tape or text-to-voice technologies, and notetakers. Some programs work to devise alternate test formats. For example, students who have particular difficulty with multiple choice items might be able to take a short essay format test. In my experience, changing the overall format of a test depends largely on the professor's willingness to work actively with disability support services.

For students who need books on tape, the Reading Foundation for the Blind and Dyslexic (RFB&D) offers a huge assortment of taped books for a nominal fee. Check out their website at www.rfbd.org. Although many institutions belong to RFB&D, I recommend that students join individually. Personal membership is available for a nominal fee.

Working with RFB&D requires advance planning. Halfway through the semester isn't the time to ask for a textbook on tape. At my college, we encourage students who need books on tape to provide our support program with their list of books as soon as possible after registering, which is usually the previous semester. When they register for a course, students probably don't know what books will be required, so they need to seek out the professor of the course and ask for that information. Even if they cannot find out through the professor, the campus bookstore will have a list of required books for specific classes, usually weeks before the class is offered.

Many DS programs also make their own texts on tape by hiring readers. A well-staffed DS office may be able to keep up with the required schedule of reading on the syllabus. While advance planning is always helpful, this service sometimes provides a last-minute solution, as long as the student can live with getting one chapter at a time. The disadvantage to this is a lack of quality control. The recording instruments are unlikely to be of studio quality and there may be problems with the reader's style, voice, or even ability.

Many students wait until they're in a crisis to use support services. That's too bad, because most programs can help students avoid those crises by providing assistance with study skills, time management, organization, writing, tutoring, and so on. However, as with almost everything at college, it's up to the student to set up and use these services.

On the other hand, I have witnessed students who seem to live in our DS office. As much as our staff encourages students to be independent, enabling relationships may be hard to avoid. Staff members tend to be empathetic; it's hard to say no when a student appears to need help desperately. Nevertheless, the consequences may be detrimental. When we surveyed our faculty about their perceptions of the DS program, one faculty member commented that he was concerned that some students seemed to be "majoring" in the program. That is, the program had become the center of their college experience. Please remember, there is more to college life than the DS office.

The goal of almost any program is to help students become effective self-advocates. Consequently, many programs emphasize skills that foster greater independence such as training students in learning strategies and helping them to understand the nature of their own learning disabilities. A good service provider will try to avoid the role of "helper and expert" who comes to the rescue. Instead, she or he should act as a facilitator who will empower the student to become a successful decision maker and problem solver.

DS staff wants students with learning disabilities to become more independent as they progress through college or university. In a like manner, students should need the DS office less as they figure out how to fend for themselves. The real goal of a good program reminds me of an old commercial for Clearasil, an acne medication that's still around today: "We want to lose you as a customer."

## Deciphering Psychoeducational Evaluations

Here's something that surprised me about the bright, well-educated, and generally successful students with learning disabilities at my college: when they first arrive at college, most of them know very little about their learning disabilities, or at least what their evaluations say about their learning disabilities. They have never sat down with the reports of their evaluations. In most cases, they've been tested several times. They know that they have learning disabilities, but they rarely know the details. They don't recognize their strengths and weaknesses, nor do they really understand how their learning disabilities affect them, both in and out of the classroom.

Reviewing and understanding psychoeducational evaluations is one of the most important things students can do to help themselves in school and in life. While reviewing documentation is especially important once a student with learning disabilities enters college, students, parents, and guidance counselors may want to start the process of reviewing evaluations with the student in high school or even earlier. It may be especially beneficial to compare and contrast previous reports with the most current versions.

Students cannot effectively advocate for themselves if they don't understand what they need — and what they don't need. In the past, someone else may have been responsible for determining what the student needed. Most college students, however, want to be more independent and this means having a clear understanding of their learning disabilities.

I have developed an independent study project for students at my college, where students earn academic credit by learning more about themselves. The project revolves around students developing a working understanding of their psychoeducational evaluations. They begin by going through their evaluations sub-test by sub-test. I ask them to summarize the evaluator's explanations (often further interpreted by a staff member trained in interpreting test results) and then to agree or disagree with the findings. One student, JJ, analyzed the subtests making up the two main components of the WAIS: verbal and performance. JJ provided a brief description of each subtest, how he fared, what the result meant, and his reaction. For example, he wrote:

> The Object Assembly subtest requires the student to put together puzzles in a timed environment. It measures perceptual organization, visual-motor coordination, ability to synthesize concrete parts into a meaningful whole, and visual perception of minimal or non-meaningful parts. My scaled score was the lowest of all my subtests and fell in the borderline range.

> I find that this subtest best describes the difficulties I have in my educational pursuits.... This impacts my ability to understand how certain events lead up to an event; an example would be sitting in history class and being instructed on the events leading up to a battle or a war. It would be difficult for me to make the necessary connection without the benefit of instruction.... I do have difficulty seeing the relationships of parts to a whole and need professors to provide direction in the form of class objectives and daily summaries to assist my comprehension and understanding of material presented....

Visual-motor weaknesses impact my writing and copying abilities. When large quantities of information are required for me to copy from a blackboard or overhead projector, it takes additional time for me to copy. Also, my handwriting has never won awards for presentation. Perceptual organization weaknesses impact my ability to write in a logical, sequential manner. Last year I was provided with the assistance of an individual to write my oral responses since I am stronger with verbal skills in comparison to my written abilities.

You may wonder how JJ, a sophomore in college, developed such a thorough understanding of the purpose of a psychological test. Actually, I happen to know that this student did not know much about the testing process prior to reviewing his own evaluation. He could have ascertained this information by looking at the manual that is used with the WAIS. He certainly could have sat down with a staff member who would have been able to explain the purpose of the testing. In this case, all it took was him reading the commentary in the report. In the majority of evaluations I have read, it's standard practice to describe each subtest in this manner. Nevertheless, this student went beyond the report itself and related it to his personal experiences.

Melanie, a junior, drew remarkably similar conclusions from analyzing her evaluation report:

Scores on the WJ-R (Woodcock Johnson Tests of Cognitive Ability- revised) dealing with perceptual organization, visual processing and visual motor abilities help me understand why I have visual spatial

71

processing difficulties. For instance, when I am assigned a paper, I can have lots of great ideas, but it's very hard to organize them. Another example is the fact that I keep my room in a certain organizational scheme: If something is moved out of its place, I am upset. This is an effort to compensate for visual organization weakness.

Melanie also did something that I encourage students to do if so moved: She disagreed with some aspects of her evaluation. For instance, she scored 85 on her intelligence test (WJ-R), a score that may be interpreted to mean that more than 80 percent of all people are "smarter" than she is. She discussed this score with the evaluator and learned that "the 85 was not reflective of my abilities and I am much more capable than the numbers suggest. I have been reassured to know this. It has given me additional confidence in my abilities."

Melanie discovered that reviewing her entire evaluation report was not a futile attempt to decipher a foreign language. Naturally, she did not understand everything in the report; I would not expect any student to have that kind of clarity. However, she was able to make sense of all sorts of useful information that helped her improve her awareness of how she learns. "Although I don't understand all of these scores," she admits, "reviewing (the evaluator's) comments while looking at the scores and thinking about my experiences in college has helped me come to a greater self-understanding."

The final piece of this first component of the independent study project is for the student to create a list of strengths. In most cases, the student has probably given plenty of attention to weaknesses. And as much as a good evaluation report should identify strengths, many reports don't give adequate consideration to what the student does well, nor do reports generally help students figure out how to use their strengths to compensate for weaknesses. I don't anticipate that the student will necessarily find a complete listing of strengths in the report. Rather, this is an opportunity for very personal reflection, a time to self-assess and provide a dimension that the evaluation may have missed.

For example, when Melanie thought about her strengths, she shared that she has a good memory for things she sees and hears, a trait that was evident in her testing. But she also included characteristics that standardized tests rarely address. She cited her sense of humor, her determination, her willingness to listen and take advice, her loyalty as a friend, and her ability to follow through on tasks and jobs.

It's vital for students to become aware of their strengths, even if they don't seem, at first glance, to have much to do with classroom performance. Everything that Melanie mentioned can (and did) help her to be successful. You might say that she discovered that she has a high level of emotional intelligence, which a number of researchers believe is more predictive of success than traditional notions of intelligence.

JJ was able to apply his newfound knowledge from some of the WAIS subtests in analyzing why he has difficulty in some classes. Perhaps more importantly, he also increased his awareness of strategies and methods to help him be successful. JJ's reflection follows:

In a lecture setting, I have difficulty extracting the most crucial information or message during the class. I will make notes of information that isn't vital to a full understanding of the issues being discussed. I have difficulty determining the main idea of lectures, movies, literature, and speeches. Due to this weakness, I tend to focus on the small details that lead up to the conclusion, which evades me.

Also, this weakness impacts my ability to problem solve. I can complete the problem solution, but usually need more time to be successful since I spend more time than the average student weeding out the relevant information needed to solve the problem. Again, I tend to become occupied with the irrelevant details rather than the details needed to solve the problem.

Since I have the tendency to ignore crucial details, when I review a paper in a testing situation, it's not uncommon for me to feel that nothing is missing. In reality, the main idea or the most crucial element of the response could be missing, yet I might provide a response with all the details leading up to the conclusion and not realize that the most important element isn't included. Since memory is a weakness for me, I must write down important dates and data. When I arrive home and need to remember crucial deadlines and information, I cannot rely on my memory since with the passing of a short period of time, I have lost the information. I must rely on a buddy in the classroom for assistance or else write down all the important information.

In addition, when information is presented in a visual manner, which is more of a strength for me, I still must copy the information and review it several times before it becomes a part of my long-term memory. This processing deficit has a significant impact on my understanding of the lectures and readings at college.

Another student, Mick, came up with an overall plan to determine how to cope with different courses in college. In a particularly tough biology class, the professor seemed to rush the lecture, gave timed quizzes at the beginning of class, and scheduled three hour labs, too long a time for Mick to stay focused. Mick decided to lay the groundwork for a more successful experience by advocating for himself.

To get around these difficulties, I talked things over with my professor, and he agreed to let me take different quizzes (at the DS office). I also obtained a notetaker for the course, so that between the two of us I wouldn't miss details in the lectures. In addition, my counselor arranged for me to get another lab partner, who had a learning disability like myself. This proved beneficial to both of us because we worked well together and gave one another support. These approaches were helpful to me and I was able to get an A- for the course, two whole letter grades higher than what I thought I would get, exceeding my expectations.

Mick concluded that he was more likely to be successful in classes that emphasized student-teacher discussions. These classes were less boring and more interactive. He could learn from and compare his perspective with other students. This type of class gave him more opportunities to demonstrate his ability to the professors. On the other hand, he learned that classes that meet for more than three hours per week took too much time away from his other studies and prevented him from registering for all the credits he wanted. He also tried not to schedule two classes consecutively to prevent problems with using extended time on tests. He concluded that he made the right decision to major in sociology, because most classes in that department met his criteria for success.

I love reading the papers from the students who take this independent study. It's fascinating to learn about them in such personal detail. Many of the students use this as an opportunity to look back on their lives as a whole, often reflecting on the struggles they have encountered growing up with learning disabilities. In many cases, they realize that they are still a little angry about the way they had been treated throughout school.

A student named Josh relates an experience that is typical of many of his peers with learning difficulties:

> I also used to hate report card day because everyone would want to know what everyone got. I remember all my friends getting all A's and some B's and I used to get C's and a couple of B's. It got to the point where I was labeled as the bad kid who never tried/cared about school. This wasn't the case at all. There comes a time when you finally just give up and start acting out the role that people give you. I think I acted out to divert attention from the fact that I didn't know the answer to the question the teacher asked....
>
> No matter how much I studied or how much I tried, I just couldn't do much better in school. My grades were still not good and my behavior wasn't

any better. After a really bad freshman year (in high school), I practically begged my parents to put me on medication. I was just so frustrated and I was tired of being the only kid in the class who didn't understand or the kid who always got the lowest grade. I would watch everyone else and wonder why they could get it and I couldn't.

I'm sure that it was painful for Josh to write about and relive his experiences, but I believe it helped him clarify a number of issues. It also gave him an opportunity to see how far he has come. In getting a better sense of himself, he has become a better self-advocate — more focused, more knowledgeable, and more confident.

Sometimes, students reveal that their learning disabilities were not the only thing that made succeeding in school difficult. Several students revealed that depression and anxiety disorders had plagued them as they were growing up. Alice recounted:

By eighth grade I was becoming severely depressed and I would have panic attacks on the way to school almost every day. I would not get out of bed without my parents being both forceful and encouraging.... I remember being terrified of high school, and finally after much discussion and hesitation on my part, my parents decided that I needed therapy. This helped my self-confidence improve a bit and I felt more secure with another adult on my side....

By the time I was in twelfth grade, my depression was completely out of control and in

November of that year I ended up hitting rock bottom and actually ended up leaving school for two months.

Alice was courageous to disclose such intimate details, and her courage helped her in a practical sense as well. As a freshman at our college, she had not interacted with DS, but after almost "hitting the wall" as a sophomore, she realized she needed help to succeed. She decided to advocate for herself. She brought evaluation reports she had never looked at to the DS office and also shared much of her personal history with the staff psychologist. The psychologist listened, looked at her report, and then described Alice as if he had known her all her life. By examining not only her learning disabilities but her depression as well, Alice and the psychologist were able to clarify what she could do to be successful in school and beyond.

## Goal Planning

Using research on highly successful adults with learning disabilities, I have developed a tool to help students get in control of their academic lives. Known as the Goal Planning Program, this tool goes beyond simply setting academic goals. Having a goal is like a New Year's resolution; it usually doesn't last more than a few days or weeks. Instead, the Goal Planning Program helps students develop strategies to achieve their goals. I designed this program as a result of working with students with and without learning disabilities who were having serious academic difficulty. It focuses on two areas that are critical for success in college:

organization and time management. The more I used the program with students, the more I discovered that it's also useful for any student who wants to have better control of his or her academic life.

### Goal planning involves the following three basic steps:

### Step 1: Looking Back

When I meet in an initial advising session with students who are not doing well (or want to do better), many are prepared with a litany of excuses or outside sources of blame for their performance. Others appear to have little idea, or at least are reluctant to admit, why they are having such academic difficulty. Some even try to deny that they are doing poorly. Consequently, I begin advising sessions with a semester assessment. After emphasizing that we are here to work together on what I assume is the common goal of academic improvement, I ask students the following questions:

- What is your overall reaction to last semester or how did you feel about it?
- What was good about it?
- What was bad about it?
- Why did you have academic difficulty?
- What could you have done differently?
- What will you do to improve in the coming semester?
- Why do you want to improve?
- How have you been successful?
- What is your outlook or goal(s) for the coming semester?

We then review the semester assessment and use this information to create a document that the student receives. We discuss how the student's responses can help us work not only on setting goals but on developing strategic planning to meet those goals. Students are more likely to understand how they may succeed when they take into account both their strengths and weaknesses, and own up to personal accountability for their actions.

Many students are willing to admit that their poor performance is a result of simply not working hard enough. Often, students have more difficulty describing their strengths than their weaknesses. The self-assessment provides me the opportunity to offer gentle confrontation. However, while working harder almost always helps, the student may also need to look at more effective ways of studying. With students who have done a semester assessment for a prior semester (which means they continue to be experiencing serious academic difficulty), I compare past and present issues. Often the remarks are similar, which leads me to ask, "You can talk the talk. Are you ready to walk the walk?"

## Step Two: Filling Out the Goal Planning Program

We begin our follow-up advising sessions by working on the Goal Planning Program form (see Exhibit 2.2). We use a program plan sheet that lays out a semester plan to meet operationally defined and measurable goals and objectives. Goal planning begins with asking the student to articulate a purpose for being in college, starting with the quintessential existentialist question, "Why am I here?" Although some students sit in stunned silence, and many admit that they have never given much thought to this question, most are able to respond. Oftentimes, the responses are the stock answers: "To graduate," "To get a good job," "Because my parents expect me to be." I encourage students to think beyond these external reasons. Do they find college enjoyable? If so, what makes it enjoyable or special?

College means more to students when they truly assess why they have made the *choice* to be there. Of course, some students do communicate an inspiring sense of purpose. A student once told me: "I love being at (our college). I'm the first person in my family to graduate high school. I feel blessed to be here. My success is important to my whole family." The goal setting process had already begun for this student.

We then examine long- and short-term goals and set an ambitious yet realistic grade goal for each course. Students need to assess both strengths/supports and weaknesses/obstacles that may affect the outcome in each class. The semester assessment again provides useful information for students who have been able to analyze aspects of their learning style. For example, students who prefer classes that involve discussion, participation, and various forms of experiential learning are not as attracted to traditional lecture style classes. Some students feel they do better on papers than objective tests, or vice versa. They may be more confident about classes that offer many evaluation opportunities as opposed to only a midterm and a final. When possible, students should match their learning preferences with course selection, which, clearly, isn't always an option. Nevertheless, an awareness that some courses present more obstacles than others can help students develop learning and studying strategies.

### Step Three: Checking in Throughout the Semester

The back of the Goal Planning Program form lists each course in a column with the weeks of the semester as rows (see Exhibit 2.3). Most course syllabi provide the due dates of requirements, particularly tests, papers, projects, and presentations. By going through each syllabus, students use the grid for further time management (I call it macro-time management) by writing down, in red, all the requirements due for each course in the appropriate week blocks. In doing so, students create a schedule of all requirements for the semester at a glance. They monitor all progress toward their grade objectives by recording every grade received in each class. By following through with their goal planning, they assume a significant degree of accountability and autonomy. This is yet another form of self-advocacy that might just improve grades as well.

## Exhibit 2.2. Goal Planning Program

Name: _____ Date: _____

**Purpose** (Why am I at this school right now?):_____
_____
_____

**Goals:**
    1. Personal _____

    2. G.P.A.
        Anticipated:_____     Required by contract: _____

## Individual Course Objectives:

|   | Course | Grade Objective | Study Time | Strengths to meet grade objective | Obstacles to meeting grade objective |
|---|--------|-----------------|------------|-----------------------------------|--------------------------------------|
| 1 |        |                 |            |                                   |                                      |
| 2 |        |                 |            |                                   |                                      |
| 3 |        |                 |            |                                   |                                      |
| 4 |        |                 |            |                                   |                                      |

## Exhibit 2.3. Progress In Courses

| | Course 1 | Course 2 | Course 3 | Course 4 | Course 5 |
|---|---|---|---|---|---|
| Wk 1 | | | | | |
| Wk 2 | | | | | |
| Wk 3 | | | | | |
| Wk 4 | | | | | |
| Wk 5 | | | | | |
| Wk 6 | | | | | |
| Wk 7 | | | | | |
| Wk 8 | | | | | |
| Wk 9 | | | | | |
| Wk 10 | | | | | |
| Wk 11 | | | | | |
| Wk 12 | | | | | |
| Wk 13 | | | | | |
| Wk 14 | | | | | |
| Wk 15 | | | | | |
| **Final grade** | | | | | |

ରେ

# Developing and Building Study Skills

## You Gotta Have a Plan, Stan

I meet with students all the time who are having academic difficulty. Many of these students tell me that they don't know how to study. I used to wonder how they did well enough in high school to get accepted at a selective college without knowing how to study. Surely they had to study in high school, I reasoned. In fact, many of these students tell me that they didn't have to study in high school! For some reason, they just got good grades. They were bright, and they didn't cause a lot of trouble. In many cases, their teachers assumed they would do well, a seemingly self-fulfilling prophecy. They never had to worry about taking notes. Anything the teacher said was already in the book. Besides, they really didn't need to read the book if they just paid enough attention in class. The questions that would be on the tests were so obvious. To be successful, all they really had to do was show up. Writing papers was hardly more of a challenge. As long as they wrote in complete sentences and could spell decently, they were just about guaranteed an A. Students with learning disabilities may have an additional disadvantage in college if, having received so much support in high school, they don't know how to take care of them-selves. They've acquired learned helplessness.

High school isn't always so easy. Many students do enter college well prepared in terms of knowing how to study; but, for a considerable number of students, the preceding scenarios are all too familiar. In a funny way, students who struggled in high school are at an advantage over those who didn't have to work hard. Those to whom success in high school did not come easily arrive at college ready to work. Moreover, they know a thing or two about how to study. They know not to wait until the night before a midterm to start reading the text or borrow someone's notes.

And yet many college-bound students with learning disabilities come to college or university without a true sense of how to study, particularly with the increased demands of postsecondary education. In some cases, they were like the other bright students, and high school was pretty easy and undemanding. Others did a great deal of work, but at the end of it all, they did not have systems or strategies for studying. Perhaps they had received so much support that things were done for them and they never learned to take care of themselves. Or they might have received accommodations, such as open book tests, that are unlikely to fly in college. It's pretty difficult to know how to study for a test if your whole prior experience with tests has been open book.

In this chapter on developing and building study skills, I look at studying in a very broad sense. To me, studying is pretty much everything a student does in order to learn; it's not simply cramming the night before a test. I have tried to break down study skills into the major components that are important for college students and will discuss these components within the context of students with learning disabilities. Remain mindful that there really are no such things as "LD study skills." There are simply sound approaches to studying that are useful to all students. They may be even more important for students with learning disabilities.

## Planning and Organization

The foundation for developing a sound approach to studying is planning and organization, particularly time management. The problem for many students is that, although they may know the right ways to study, their organizational skills are so poor that they never get around to it.

Total disorganization seems to be a rite of passage for many college students, especially guys. Have you ever been in a guy's dorm room? It makes John Belushi's room in *Animal House* look like a Martha Stewart creation. It might be a total mess, but so what? This is college. There are no rules about picking up your clothes or making the bed. Students can wear the same shirt and shorts for days on end — maybe even underwear, but I don't want to go there. I see my share of students who go to bed in the wee hours of the morning and rise in time for a late lunch. When they do occasionally get to class, they don't know what's going on. They have no idea of where they're supposed to be in the reading. They're lucky if they remember there's a test or paper due a day in advance. In the long run, this lifestyle generally does not lead to success. For students with learning disabilities, this behavior leads to disaster.

### Taking Control

From my experiences with successful adults with learning disabilities, being in control of life is the key to success in college and beyond. If you're disorganized, whether it be with housework, returning phone calls, doing holiday shopping, or any of the seemingly infinite tasks of daily life, I'll bet at some level you think that things are out of control. When things are out of control for college students with learning disabilities, stress, frustration, and struggle generally follow. These students must get organized. I won't clean up rooms, but I will provide tools to help with studying. I've mentioned some general ways that students can organize themselves in the section on goal planning. Here I will try to give more step-by-step advice.

Let's start with the first day of class. Instructors generally hand out the infamous syllabus for the course. They might even go over it during the first class. This is the first chance to do some organizing. While looking over the requirements and timelines, students might want to ask the basic question: "Can I handle this?" Although it's rare, some students are able to determine that they really should not be taking a course just by looking at the requirements on the syllabus. I almost always counsel students not to make hasty or impulsive decisions. They should at least speak with the instructor about their concerns and probably try out a few class sessions. There is something to be said, however, about coming to a decision quickly. If it's clear that the class is too much or that it's just a terrible fit, the student who gets out early (usually within the first week) has time to find another class to replace it.

Having said all that, I think students, and especially students with learning disabilities, tend to overreact or freak out too easily on the first day of class. "There's NO WAY I can do all this, all these readings, tests, papers, projects." Hold on, bud. It may be a lot of work, but most students probably can handle it. They need to start with a plan, and that dreaded syllabus is actually a helpful ally.

## Macro Time Management

The Progress in Courses plan, Exhibit 2.3, on the back of the Goal Planning Program, Exhibit 2.2, provides an extremely easy way to turn the syllabus into a useful aid. A student generally needs no more than ten minutes to write down virtually all the requirements in all courses. In ten minutes, the student has created an organizational plan for the entire semester – on one piece of paper. Some analysis is needed to make the grid more helpful. Each row represents a week. Students should take a look at how the weeks flow from one to the other. In weeks where all or almost all the cells have something in them, advance planning and preparation are critical. If only one cell in a given week has something in it, the student can handle this week as it comes up. There are exceptions, of course. For example, if the requirement is a term paper, the student will need to start it before the week it's due.

This Progress in Courses plan offers a number of benefits for students. First, they don't need to thumb through all their stuff to find a syllabus and then thumb through the syllabus to find the assignment and when it's due. By using this plan, students will never be in doubt about what they have to do. I encourage students to put this piece of paper in a place where they will see it frequently. If they have a notebook that they use for all courses, they should tape the plan to the inside of the front cover. If they work regularly at the desk in their room, they might tape it to the desk or the wall in front of the desk. Some students like to tape it to the inside of their door, so that they always see it as they leave their room. By glancing at it frequently, they will find that they internalize their schedule; they know when things are due; they are able to plan and organize more effectively because they have a much better sense of what they need to get done.

Students should also use this chart to keep track of how they are doing in their classes. Whenever a quiz, test, paper, or project is handed back, they write down the grade next to it on the chart. When I have asked students why they failed or did not do well in a class, you would not believe how many times I hear, "Uh, I thought I was doing OK." When they chart their own progress, they will never be surprised.

If students see that they are not doing well or not meeting their goals in a class, they can take measures to improve their performance before it's too late. It's not a matter of failure; it's recognizing the need to do something different. Talking about difficulties early on with instructors or staff at DS is a sensible first step in figuring out how to change the approach to the class.

When students are doing well and meeting their own goals, writing down their grades provides concrete, positive reinforcement. They may never again look at that A test, but they'll see the grade every time they look at their chart and will be reminded that success is possible.

## Micro Time Management

The Progress in Courses Sheet gives the big picture, a kind of macro time management tool. Students also need to focus on the day-to-day. The place to start is a daily-weekly planner, essentially a personal calendar that lives in and out of the student's backpack. It should include all course requirements as listed on the Progress in Courses chart, as well as the academic calendar for the current semester. Amazingly, many students don't know where to find an academic calendar, even though it's readily available in a course catalog, the course registration bulletin, or plenty of other sources. These days, the college or university website almost always provides the academic calendar and is a great resource for finding out what's going on in general.

Using the academic calendar, the student writes down important dates (semester breaks, exam periods, class registration for the next semester, etc.) in his or her daily-weekly planner. Thus seeing the heavy work periods, the student can make more realistic decisions about how to allocate time. I even recommend *some* social planning. Most institutions have an events calendar or all inclusive calendar that list concerts, performances, lectures, games, and so on. Getting organized might be the way to get tickets to the best concerts and events.

The final component for effective time management, the Daily-Weekly Schedule, is seen in Exhibit 2.4. This schedule is different than a daily-weekly planner and can be completed in only a few minutes. It does not address specific assignments and requirements. Rather, it sets out a weekly routine that should be as consistent as possible.

In a sense, college students aren't asked to do much. They generally have only twelve to twenty scheduled hours of class per week, leaving plenty of time left over for... for...? Some students just seem to know what to do with all this so-called free time. But many students quickly become victims of having too much unorganized time. It doesn't take a rocket scientist to know that college life is chaotic. The antidote to this chaos is to establish a routine, which begins with the one structured element of the week, the class schedule. I tell students to fill out the Daily-Weekly Schedule (Exhibit 2.4), beginning with their class schedule as follows:

- Box in the times and days of classes.
- Label every class block.
- Box in other activities that are scheduled or predictable, including:
  — meals,
  — job,
  — sports,
  — clubs or activities,
  — working out,
  — just hanging.

Next, the student plans out the time needed per week to keep up with each class. Goal planning involves estimating how much study time per week outside of class will be necessary to achieve each grade objective. Although the average college student spends less than fifteen hours per week studying, the rule of thumb for a typical college course is to spend two hours outside of class for every hour in class. Students who routinely allot this time to their studies vastly increase their odds of being successful. Armed with this breakdown of how time should be spent during the week, students are ready to create a daily schedule.

## Exhibit 2.4. Daily-Weekly Schedule
### Week Of _____

|          | Monday | Tuesday | Wednesday | Thursday | Friday | Saturday | Sunday |
|----------|--------|---------|-----------|----------|--------|----------|--------|
| 5:00am   |        |         |           |          |        |          |        |
| 6:00     |        |         |           |          |        |          |        |
| 7:00     |        |         |           |          |        |          |        |
| 8:00     |        |         |           |          |        |          |        |
| 9:00     |        |         |           |          |        |          |        |
| 10:00    |        |         |           |          |        |          |        |
| 11:00    |        |         |           |          |        |          |        |
| 12:00pm  |        |         |           |          |        |          |        |
| 1:00     |        |         |           |          |        |          |        |
| 2:00     |        |         |           |          |        |          |        |
| 3:00     |        |         |           |          |        |          |        |
| 4:00     |        |         |           |          |        |          |        |
| 5:00     |        |         |           |          |        |          |        |
| 6:00     |        |         |           |          |        |          |        |
| 7:00     |        |         |           |          |        |          |        |
| 8:00     |        |         |           |          |        |          |        |
| 9:00     |        |         |           |          |        |          |        |
| 10:00    |        |         |           |          |        |          |        |
| 11:00    |        |         |           |          |        |          |        |
| 12:00am  |        |         |           |          |        |          |        |

Notes:

The time required to be a successful student is about the same as working a full-time job. Figuring twelve to fifteen hours per week in class, and doubling that time for studying, gives a grand total from thirty-six to forty-five hours. In other words, it's a regular work week. Almost every student I've known has worked a forty hour per week job at some point. They say it's not a problem to put in forty hours. I really like to focus on a Monday to Friday schedule, an approach that encourages students to take a more business-like attitude toward their studies. At the same time, my experience has indicated that expecting students to do a great deal of work on Friday afternoon is generally not realistic. For most students, weekends do become part of their workweek in allocating study time.

I ask students to treat college like a job. Students who spend 40 hours per week on their courses will not only be successful students, they will still have 128 hours leftover each week. Take away 56 for sleeping, and that's 72 for fun!

A student, Jason, maps out his schedule as follows: First, he estimates hours of study time per week. Figuring on eight hours for English, five hours for sociology, four hours for music appreciation, and ten hours for biology, Jason determines he will spend twenty-seven hours per week studying. At eight hours per week, English breaks down into four two-hour sessions per week. Consequently, he looks at his daily schedule and blocks out these four two-hour sessions around classes and scheduled activities on four different days. These four blocks for English are now part of his schedule. He schedules the remainder of study time similarly. Exhibit 2.5 shows Jason's daily schedule.

## Exhibit 2.5. Jason's Daily Schedule
### Week Of _____

| | Monday | Tuesday | Wednesday | Thursday | Friday | Sat. | Sun. |
|---|---|---|---|---|---|---|---|
| 5:00am | | | | | | | |
| 6:00 | | | | | | | |
| 7:00 | | | | | | | |
| 8:00 | | | | | | | |
| 9:00 | English Class | | English Class | | English Class | | |
| 10:00 | Study Music | Sociology Class | Study Music | Sociology Class | Study Music | | |
| 11:00 | Music Appreciation Class | | Music Appreciation Class | | Music Appreciation Class | | |
| 12:00pm | LUNCH | LUNCH | LUNCH | LUNCH | LUNCH | | |
| 1:00 | Biology Class | | Biology Class | Study Music | Biology Class | | |
| 2:00 | Study Biology | Biology Lab | Study Biology | Study Biology | Study Music and/or Sociology as needed | | |
| 3:00 | | | | | | | |
| 4:00 | Break | | Break | Break | | | |
| 5:00 | Study Biology | Break | Study Biology | Study Biology | | | |
| 6:00 | | | | | | | |
| 7:00 | Study English | Study English | Study English | Study English | | | |
| 8:00 | | | | | | | |
| 9:00 | | | | | | | |
| 10:00 | | | | | | | |
| 11:00 | | | | | | | |
| 12:00am | | | | | | | |

Notes:

Many students like to highlight the boxes according to an organizational color scheme. Some use one color for classes, another for study time, and another for activities. Others use a different color for each course, with study time the same color as its respective class. Some students don't color-code at all. Whatever floats your boat!

Two Suggestions for Effective Scheduling:

1.  Make use of morning and afternoon time. Most students wait until the evening to get to their studying, and then feel they never have enough time. Look at all the time in a day; an hour here between classes in the morning, two hours there, or maybe just forty-five minutes after lunch before the next class. What do students do with this time — watch TV? They can make better use of their time. The great thing about getting in an hour or so of studying in the morning is that it's pretty painless. There is only a limited amount of time; don't expect to write a twenty page paper, just figure on reading a few pages. Before you know it, the time's up, and you move on.

2.  Study times should consist of chunks of forty-five minutes to one hour, never longer, and never more than three sessions back to back. That is, a three hour block a couple of afternoons per week should be broken into three separate sessions: fifty minutes study, fifteen minute break; fifty minutes study, fifteen minute break; fifty minutes study — time's up, done and outta here! Some students like to devote the three sessions to three different classes. Others like to stick with just one class at a time over the course of the three hours.

## Pick Up Your Room

Time management tools are only one way to help with planning and organization. Being physically organized is also important, especially for students with learning disabilities. Many persons with learning disabilities have to arrange their living space in precise ways. If anything is out of order, they are thrown off until they can get their space organized again. Some people with learning disabilities have difficulties with their visual memory. If they put something out of sight, they will not remember where they placed it. As a result, they need to keep everything they need visible.

I once spoke with a successful professional woman with learning disabilities about her kitchen. It was beautiful. Every kitchen appliance you can imagine was hanging neatly on the walls or placed on the counters. The cabinets all had glass doors. The silverware, cutlery, etc. were not in drawers but rather in open containers. I could see virtually everything in her kitchen. She explained that she *had* to see everything; if she put anything away, she would not remember where she had put it and would never find it.

Telling my kids to pick up their room has never worked well for me, but I do recommend that students with learning disabilities keep their class materials — books, notebooks, etc., in one easily accessible area. A well-organized work space in a dorm room needs to consist of nothing more than a computer, desk, small bookcase, and small file cabinet. The class materials must be organized. Most students use an individual notebook for each course; some use an all-in-one. I personally prefer and recommend individual notebooks. Among other things, they make it easier to separate the materials of one course from those of another. On the other hand, the all-in-one notebook does reduce the number of things to keep organized. The following are some organizational tips:

- Don't throw away handouts, readings, papers and tests!
- Use folders with inside pockets to organize paperwork.
- Use different folders for different types of paperwork. Put tests and papers in one, handouts in another, and readings in another.
- Label each folder.

I admit that even when I file my paperwork in labeled folders, I sometimes leave the folders lying around — and lose them! Students need to do a better job and can use shelves, a file cabinet, desk drawers, whatever makes for good storage. The key is consistency — a place for everything and everything in its place. The goal is to develop a study routine, and having organized materials is the first step.

Although students may claim that they can study in their rooms, I doubt that's the case. Instead, I present the Top Ten reasons not to study in a dorm room:

10. Roommate plays (fill in the blank music) too loudly.
9. Roommate hangs out with boyfriend, girlfriend, rugby team drinking champ, etc.
8. Roommate is boyfriend, girlfriend, rugby team drinking champ, etc.

7. Hall mates check in with a "Wuzzup" every 15 minutes.

6. The party across the hall.

5. The party that just broke out in your room.

4. The nightly fire alarm and evacuation.

3. There's always something good on TV.

2. Even if there's not, ever hear of DVDs?

And the number one reason not to study in a dorm room...

1. One word — PlayStation.

There are exceptions. Some students with learning disabilities are assigned a single room as an accommodation to limit the distractions of dorm life. I have even seen some "quiet dorms" where students do study in their rooms, respect the need for quiet for their neighbors, and take their rowdiness outside the dorm. But, in general, studying in one's dorm room is asking for trouble.

### A Home Away from Home

The libraries at most colleges and universities offer a number of excellent places to study. On the other hand, the college library may also be a social hub. Students need to make a conscious effort to find a spot in the library that is free of distractions. Some students like to find those out-of-the-way places in a library, burying themselves deep in the stacks where no one visits. Generally, study carrels give desk space and privacy. Many students avoid these study spaces because they look too lonely or austere. Again, to be a successful student, especially with learning disabilities, requires discipline. An isolated space can be a comfortable, personal one.

Students carry around a lifetime collection of their music on an iPod the size of a credit card. As I write this, I'm listening to my music on my computer. It helps me escape into my own world and stay focused on my task. Students with learning disabilities need to understand their levels of distractibility. Some people can study with any kind of music at any of volume. Others prefer classical, jazz, new age, or soft background music. Highly distractible students with learning disabilities may profit from ambient or white noise, that is, a low level sound that essentially blocks out other distracting sounds in the environment. Similar and often preferable are recordings such as "relaxing sounds," and "sounds of nature," which create steady and soothing background sounds.

When I was a student, I liked to go to different areas of the library to do different kinds of work. As an English literature major, I had tons of reading to do. I made this work much more pleasant by going to one of the many small reading rooms/lounges scattered about the library. I would settle into an overstuffed easy chair and would remind myself that the literature I was reading was, at least in its own era, entertaining. However, I tended to read textbooks at a desk or carrel, where it was easier to spread out materials and take notes. I found that I associated different work styles with different areas. Reading literature was relatively laid back and pleasant; textbook reading and writing papers required a more disciplined approach.

I also discovered that it was psychologically beneficial for me to separate my work space (the library) from my non-work space (my room). When I walked through the library doors, it was like clocking in at work. I was ready to go. And when I left the library, I left my work behind, to the extent that that's possible for a college student. By following a regular study schedule, I knew that I was keeping up with my work. It did require self-discipline to get myself to the library several times a day, but when I walked out at night, I knew I could relax. I had done what I needed to do. I came to love the library, even though I could not bring in my music. The walkman hadn't even been invented!

## Keep it all in Perspective

I'm not saying students shouldn't have any fun in college. Hey, I know, students just want to have fun. Some of this partying is what we remember most from college — it's a rite of passage. Much learning takes place in the most unexpected ways outside of the classroom. I learned that my stomach would not put up with six beers in half an hour. I actually lost the urge to drink like that by the end of my freshman year! I encourage students to stay on track and assure them that fun will find them. It's pretty hard to miss a party on most college campuses. The keys are moderation and keeping priorities straight.

For some students with learning disabilities, being overly organized, disciplined and focused can be a liability, turning them into control freaks. They've used planners since elementary school and have organized all important events in their lives for the next four years. Being responsible and in control is important, but let's take it down a notch. I've seen students freak out if they get off their schedule at all. Guess what? It's inevitable. It's going to happen, and it needn't be the end of the world. The successful student with learning disabilities is organized but also flexible.

### In Class

Perhaps no other element of the academic experience is more significant than time spent in class. Unfortunately, many students think that just showing up to class is all they have to do. Of course attending class is critical, but it's not enough. Good students make good use of their time in class.

Here's what I tell students:

**1. Go to all classes, every day.**

a. Whenever possible, schedule classes at times that are feasible: 8 a.m. classes are not for everyone.

b. Going to class saves time. It takes much more time to make up for a missed class.

c. Students who miss class find it harder to understand lecture and discussion when they do attend.

**2. Get the best seat in the house.** This one ought to be a no-brainer. In general, it's easier to follow what is happening when seated at the front of the class. Yet, in most classes, the front is the last area where most students want to sit. It's kind of cool to kick back and relax in the last row. In fact, that's exactly what tends to happen. Let other students waste their time in class. Remember that warning about having to work harder than other students? Students with learning disabilities are often distractible. Limit distractions by not having to strain to hear or see what's going on.

**3. Be prepared.** Not knowing what's going on in a class is frustrating and embarrassing. The further behind one gets the less one will understand in class, and a negative spiral ensues. Many students have told me that once they start missing class and falling behind, going to class becomes increasingly aversive. They miss more and more classes, often with disastrous consequences. They may point to many reasons for their downfall, but the problem is rooted in a lack of preparation.

The easiest way to prepare for any class is to attend all the ones before it. Even students who have never opened the textbook (not recommended!) basically know what's going on if they've been in class. However, appreciation of class increases immeasurably by keeping up with the outside work, particularly readings and homework. In many cases, the professor will lecture on the reading for that class. Completing the reading beforehand provides you with some familiarity with the topic, and gives you a better context for understanding the professor's examples and tangents. It will also help you prepare for questions and discussion.

**4. Stay on task.** We've all been to classes where we just could not pay attention. This may be even more of a problem for students with learning disabilities. Characteristics of attention deficit and hyperactivity certainly make class more of a challenge. Even without a specific attention deficit, a student with learning disabilities may find that any number of possible learning difficulties (e.g., a slower rate of processing, a reading difficulty) may interfere with staying on task.

Part of staying on task is a combination of getting into a state of mind to listen and learn and then using self-discipline to stick with it. A simple reminder before every class that paying attention is part of your job will help maintain focus. Centering exercises before class such as deep breathing, meditation, or relaxation techniques, may help you pay attention, stay focused, participate, and stay actively engaged. Some students call this "putting on their game face" for class.

I urge students to periodically check in with themselves to see if they are paying attention. For example, in a class that meets from 10 to 11 o'clock, you could begin by writing down 10:10, 10:20, 10:30, 10:40, and 10:50 at the top of the notes. This is a reminder to check in with yourself at each of these times. When you are paying attention, you cross out the time and class continues. If this is not the case, you need to make an effort to regain focus. Use of such a system on a regular basis leads to more attentiveness. Monitoring your own thinking, something known as metacognition, allows for refocus.

**5. Learn note-taking strategies.** Many students with learning disabilities believe that they are not good notetakers. There certainly may be a basis for this belief, as almost any kind of learning difficulty may interfere with what is an already complex and difficult process. In order to take good notes, you must listen closely, understand what is being said, decide what is important and what is not, and write down the important ideas succinctly while still listening to new information. Good notetaking truly involves multitasking. Perhaps it's not surprising that having a notetaker is one of the most common accommodations for college students with learning disabilities.

I believe that many students with learning disabilities sell themselves short when it comes to notetaking. Many have never tried an organizational system. One of the most common systems is to use headers to create an outline, as follows:

I.  Main Topic
    A.  Subtopic
        1.  minor topic (within subtopic)
            a.  example
                i.  details

The content of a well-organized lecture will tend to unfold in this fashion. Not every part of the lecture will necessarily lead into all these levels. Some main topics will have a number of subtopics; others will only have one or two. Sometimes, even a main topic will be followed by several examples without going into sub or minor topics. Most students adapt the outlining process to make it consistent with the style of the class.

The problem that most students encounter with note taking is deciding which information is important or relevant and which is not. There are no easy answers, and to some extent such decision making requires a certain amount of guesswork. The practical question to ask is, "Does this sound like something that would be on a quiz or test?" Constantly asking such questions is another example of how meta-cognition helps with staying on task.

When is something important enough to write down? A rule of thumb is that if the professor writes something down, the student should write it down. In an era of over-heads and PowerPoint presentations, it may be virtually impossible to keep up with everything that's going on in a wired classroom. Nevertheless, the trend with technology in the classroom to provide more multi-sensory learning experiences should be good news for students with learning disabilities. And many professors who employ these new technologies routinely provide students with hardcopy handouts.

Students write down their notes in many different ways. A sizable margin provides space for writing questions or pointers later on. Some notes look fastidious; more look like a Jackson Pollock original. Trying to keep notes neat is always helpful. Notes won't do much good if you can't read them.

Students who use a laptop in class generate notes that are guaranteed to look great. Excellent keyboarding skills are necessary to make laptop note taking effective. The ability to touch type is an advantage because eye contact with the instructor, board, or screen can be maintained while taking notes. Word processing makes reorganizing notes relatively simple and many programs can organize and format notes automatically.

Students who cannot take notes well while following what is going on in class may be allowed to use a notetaker as an accommodation. I know more than a few students who believe that if they have a notetaker they can just sit back and comfortably absorb the lecture or discussion. Wrong. Even with a notetaker, you should take some kind of notes, even if you just write down the main ideas. Taking notes is a way to keep focused and remain on task. It kicks in that metacognition stuff and forces you to *think* about what is going on in class.

Even skimpy notes should be saved. After picking up notes from the notetaker (which should happen ASAP after class), compare the notetaker's notes with your own version. Is there agreement on the main ideas or topics? Agreement tends to mean that both the notetaker and the student are on the right track. Disagreement means that someone is not. It may take a third party to help figure out who isn't tracking with the class. DS is a good place for help with such matters. If the notetaker isn't on target, a different notetaker is needed.

For many students with learning disabilities, the tape recorder offers an effective means of ensuring good notes. However, using a tape recorder efficiently means more work for you, not less. Perhaps that's why the value of recording classes is overlooked. Students with learning disabilities who accept and realize that hard work comes with the territory may find that tape-recording class is the best way to allow them to generate quality notes with maximum independence and autonomy. As long as using a tape recorder is an accommodation approved by the DS office, recording is usually allowed in class.

**6. Participate.** Americans love the strong, silent type ("Make my day" is probably Clint Eastwood's lengthiest speech). Strong is okay, but silence does not make for the best use of time in class. Almost all the college students with learning disabilities whom I've met say that they learn best in an experiential or hands-on situation. Getting involved in class discussions is the hands-on part of many classes. Lack of participation in class may cause boredom. Some instructors notice the non-participators as much as the participators. The professor may wonder if the quiet student is unprepared, not interested, or perhaps even hostile. Conversely, students who participate communicate to the professor that they are interested and motivated. A professor's favorable perception cannot hurt. Moreover, class is more interesting if you're in the game rather than on the sidelines. Nothing makes the time in class go by like a heated discussion — especially when you're in the middle of it!

Engaging in class discussion is much easier when you have prepared for class. Even so, some students are unsure about how to get involved or are nervous that they will say something dumb. I tell students who are insecure to prepare a couple of questions in advance of class. Some may be questions that are just a way of getting other students talking about a topic. In other cases, the question may come from really not understanding something in the reading or from the last class. Questions don't make you look dumb; they make you look prepared and conscientious. Besides, most professors love questions. The student who asks for a little extra explanation makes the professor look that much smarter. Never underestimate the ego of a professor. There is only one dumb question — the one you ask on the way home *after* class.

## Out of Class

### 1. Study routines

When students meet with me to set up daily schedules, I emphasize the importance of developing routines. Routines actually make us less dependent on time-management and organization techniques. We don't have to stop and think about what we're supposed to do next. We just do it.

The best way to build study routines is to start with the Daily-Weekly Schedule presented in Exhibit 2.4. Make sure that sufficient blocks of time are dedicated to studying. Start by looking at blocks that are adjacent to classes and block out study time before or after the class each day the class meets.

There are advantages to studying either right before a class or right after. For some classes, doing homework as soon as the class is over is about the only way to remember *how* to do the work. In contrast, focusing on the work at hand right before class may be helpful in the case of classes that require heavy participation or have frequent quizzes. It all depends. The important component is having an adequate routine for studying and doing homework.

You are able to schedule an hour of studying right after history class each day, that still leaves three or more hours of studying to meet the 2:1 homework/class time ratio. Consequently, you will need to schedule in three or so more hours of history study; it might be in the afternoon or evening. As with the class schedule, I'd suggest breaking these remaining hours into sixty or ninety minute blocks and scheduling them over a couple of days.

## 2. Working with DS

The DS office can be a great place to monitor and finetune time management and organization. It's one thing to have a schedule complete with a well thought-out and intentioned study routine. It's another thing to follow through and do all that needs to be done. That's where DS comes in. Generally, DS staff will meet with students on a weekly (sometimes more) basis. This weekly appointment isn't for tutoring or studying per se. It's to make sure the student is keeping up, staying on schedule, and getting the work done. A weekly appointment is a chance to check in and review the Progress in Courses sheet. The counselor and student not only discuss what work was due (and hopefully done) in the last week, but also look ahead to the following week. What work has to be done? Does the current study routine provide enough time for this week's work? Most weeks, it probably will, but in any given week, the student may need to make adjustments. Studying for a test or writing a paper usually involves more time than completing a typical week's reading assignment.

Working with a DS counselor is helpful, especially in the beginning of college, because most of us are more responsible if we know we have to report to someone. It's incredibly easy for students to fall behind and fool them-selves into believing that nothing is wrong. The counselor will not be fooled. One of the greatest benefits of self-advocacy is that it encourages individuals to face problems now, not later. Procrastination may be a pitfall for most college students, but it's exponentially more dangerous for students with learning disabilities. Using DS as part of an overall study plan allows students to gain a toehold in the never-ending fight of putting off until tomorrow what should be done today.

### 3. Study partners

Learning isn't a solitary activity. If it were, we'd hardly need teachers or classes. Most students will learn more outside of class by working with other students. Getting together with a study partner or group is sometimes the only way to understand topics and concepts from some classes. It also makes studying for tests.... well, maybe not fun, but certainly much less painful and aversive.

Students with learning disabilities may not be sure how to find study partners, especially in classes where they don't know many of the other students. Once again, self-advocacy plays a key role. It is not unusual for college classes to have contact information available for all students. For example, classes that use interactive software such as *Blackboard* allow any student to email any other student in the class. Putting out a request for a study partner or group may take a little nerve, but it's not really so difficult to put together a short email asking if anyone is interested in getting together to study. Professors may be able to make good recommendations for study partnersor may even be willing to help organize a group or groups.

You won't always have the luxury of determining the specific make-up or dynamic of a study group, but you certainly should be aware of what works best for you. I do not necessarily recommend seeking out the top student in the class who seems brainier than the professor, but rather a competent student who has to put in some elbow grease to do well. Students tend to learn more from students who have to work through the material than from students who find everything comes easily. After all, these "genius" students cannot even imagine why someone else doesn't get it. On the other hand, students who have had to struggle a little may understand why another student isn't getting it.

Study groups are particularly useful for preparing for tests. To be most efficient, a system needs to be in place. For example, if four students are in a group, each student should have an individual responsibility — perhaps outlining one fourth of the material, or coming up with practice questions on their quarter. It's always a good idea to develop practice questions. The most effective type of studying simulates the testing conditions. The more a student practices taking a test (or the study group's closest version of it), the more familiar the test itself will be. Some researchers even suggest that it's good to study in the same room where the test will be given so that all the sensations of the entire testing experience will be familiar.

## 4. Staying in control

Balance. Moderation in everything. Schedules and routines do provide a critical measure of control in an otherwise chaotic world. One of the reasons for having a schedule and routine is to make sure that you have time for everything else in life besides studying. Let's start with the basics — eating and sleeping. Want to guess how many college students don't eat or sleep on a regular basis? As much as I have great admiration for cultures that are not time oriented (eating when hungry, sleeping when tired, hunting when there's prey), college just shouldn't work that way — especially for students with learning disabilities.

The daily schedule should have routines for eating and sleeping. Skipping meals or eating at totally random times, staying up all night one night and then crashing before dinner the next — these habits are as likely to cause difficulties as skipping class or blowing off work. Not attending to basic needs is the first step in developing a life that is out of control. And basic needs, at least in my book, extend beyond eating and sleeping. We all have a need for down time, for relaxation, recreation, and socialization. It's just a matter of balance, discipline, and organization. Self-advocacy means taking care of yourself — including developing and maintaining a lifestyle that balances work and play.

## How to Study

### 1. It's Everywhere!

I like to think of studying as *everything* the student does related to a class. In class, with metacognition kicking in, you should be thinking, "Does this sound like something that will apprear on a test?" Thinking "test" during a class    gets you more focused and engaged. Thinking "test" while reading isn't a bad idea, either. The idea is to kick in metacognition at every opportunity. As you study or do homework, you need to ask yourself the following questions:

    a. Is this information important?
    b. Is this something that the instructor has talked about?

    c. Do I understand the general concept?

    d. Will I need to reread this to understand it?

    e. Will I need to memorize this?

    f. Could this be a question on a test?

Students who have heeded the previous suggestions recognize that cramming doesn't work. They use the daily schedule, have a routine and realize that studying isn't about trying to do a semester's worth of reading the night before the exam. It's a skill, a discipline, and it needs to be part of your everyday life as a college student. Once it becomes part of your daily routine, it's not really that hard to do.

### 2. Textbook reading

Anyone familiar with study skills and reading techniques has probably heard of SQ3R (developed by F. P. Robinson, 1946, in a book entitled *Effective Study: Survey, Question, Read, Recite, Review*). A number of variations on SQ3R exist. I prefer ones that devote at least one 'R' to reflection.

Rather than discuss various approaches to reading, which alone could make up an entire book, I will offer a means for reading chapters in textbooks, particularly at the college level. All books are not created equal, and texts will vary as to the type and amount of supporting material included. Students should feel free to adapt this method to a variety of reading tasks. Suggested steps include the following:

    a. Read the contents/front guide.

    b. Skim the chapter, looking at headings, bold words, etc.

c. Read the summary at the end of the chapter.

d. Try to picture what the chapter is about.

e. Make a copy of the questions at the end of the chapter and set out to answer them.

f. Start to read the chapter.

g. Look for the answer to Q1, etc.

h. As you find each answer, highlight it and write the corresponding question number in the margin.

i. After you read each section or subsection, stop and reflect on what you've read.

j. Use the questions at the end of the chapter when you study, writing down your answer without looking at the book. Check your answer by flipping to where you know the answer is.

### 3. Organizing and reviewing notes

As I've mentioned, notes should be organized and neat, which in some cases means rewriting them. Some students believe that they are studying simply by copying their notes. Don't bank on it. Studying from notes primarily involves understanding concepts, asking questions, and using the notes to verify answers. Almost any advice on notetaking encourages the use of wide margins or some kind of space to write down questions, comments, or observations. When studying for tests, you should make use of this space by writing questions adjacent to the notes with the corresponding answers. As test time gets closer, cover the notes, look at the questions, and then verify the answer in the notes.

### 4. Periodic reviewing

Reviewing notes and assigned reading material should not take place the night before (or the day of) a test. The more you look back, reflect, and let information sink in, the easier it is to prepare and study for tests. Reviewing notes or reading without the pressure of having to study for a test requires self-discipline, and is best accomplished by building review time into your study schedule. For example, if you want to review once per week for a given class you might mark out half the study block on Friday morning for this course as "review." To review on a daily basis, a student would earmark ten to fifteen minutes of a daily block for review.

## 5. THE BIG TEST

Let's face it, few things are more stressful than THE BIG TEST. On numerous occasions throughout my adult life, I have had a dream where I'm back in college, it's the day of the final exam, and I realize that I have never attended the class, have forgotten to study, or have shown up in my underwear (maybe that's a different dream). Interestingly, many adults report having similar anxiety dreams. The fact that twenty, thirty, even fifty years out of college the memory of taking big tests or exams is still a source of stress and fear for many people says something about the level of anxiety related to taking tests.

One way to beat test anxiety is to lower the fear factor, that factor being fear of the unknown. Consequently, the more familiar the student is with the testing experience, the less likely he or she is to encounter the unknown. That's why "thinking the test" a lot of the time isn't such a bad idea. Making the idea of a test part of everyday life actually decreases anxiety — a kind of systematic desensitization.

I recommend students start to prepare for a big test a week or so in advance. The initial task is just to get organized by considering what the test will cover and what notes, books, handouts, are needed. Once the materials are gathered together, I recommend skimming them as a general review. This also helps you start thinking about the content well before the test, perhaps leading to some active cogitating. If the test seems to require about six hours of serious studying, I recommend breaking it down into three daily two-hour sessions. We've already discussed approaches such as study groups and study locations. The key is test simulation. The more time you spend actively thinking about and answering questions, the more you experience testing conditions and the less likely you are to be sidelined by fear.

A big test is like a big game. Athletes do get nervous, but they also get excited. They look forward to going out, giving it their best shot, and then leaving it all on the field. And none of the successful athletes I've met go into a game thinking that they will lose. Where do they get this confidence and positive attitude? First, they are prepared. They have worked on the fundamentals and conditioning (translation to academics: going to class, keeping up with work, periodically reviewing, etc.) and they have also planned for this game (i.e., studying for the test and simulating conditions as much as possible). Students who prepare themselves for a test like athletes for a game can come to the test confident and excited, seeing it as a challenge or an opportunity to prove what they know.

Even with the best preparation, students often show up to tests with clammy palms, roiling stomachs, and trouble remembering how to breathe. I encourage students to arrive for exams five to ten minutes ahead of time; arriving too early gets the anxiety pumping, too late is just big trouble. During the few minutes prior to the test, it's helpful to do some intentional relaxation such as deep breathing, visualizations, and so on. With this preparation, students should find themselves refreshed, energized, ready to roll. It's time to get the party started.

An excellent resource for students who experience anxiety around test taking is *Test Anxiety and What You Can Do About It* by Joseph Casbarro. Filled with ideas and tips, this practical guide provides pre-test, in-test, and post-test strategies that will help you maximize your performance.

## Taking Tests
### 1. Getting in the right frame of mind and body

Adhering to a routine that minimizes disruption to everyday activities, particularly sleeping and eating, will cultivate the right frame of mind and body for a test. It also helps greatly to have a positive attitude. Tests are opportunities for you to demonstrate what you have learned. Benjamin Bloom has wondered what our educational system would be like if students had the same enthusiasm for the challenge of final exams as they do for the final football game. Most students don't get themselves psyched up about tests and exams, but if students with learning disabilities adopt a positive and competitive attitude, they are more likely to succeed.

## 2. Managing time during a test

Another common accommodation for college students with learning disabilities is extended time for test-taking. Ironically, this sometimes sets up a false expectation that students with learning disabilities don't need to manage their time. Extended time rarely means unlimited time; students generally receive time and a half or double time, rarely more. For students who process more slowly, even the extra time must be managed. Additionally, focusing on managing time usually helps students better focus on taking the test itself.

When the test is passed out, you should immediately look it over in its entirety. If the test is divided into sections, you should guesstimate the time needed for each section within the total time allotted. You should set a deadline for yourself five to ten minutes in advance of the stop time in order conduct a final review.

First attend to the sections and questions that you feel confident about. It's very important not to get bogged down, which tends to lead to rumination, negative thinking, and wasted time. It's equally important to monitor the time. Most of us are able to speed up our work if we know we are falling off pace. Knowing how the schedule is going makes it easier to decide when to skip over a particularly difficult problem in order to stay on pace.

Make sure you note any problems you skip or don't finish and come back to them after you have completed the test. If no time is left, it was still a better decision to skip those problems and focus on the easier ones.

### 3. Tips for multiple choice questions

Students can take entire skill-building courses on how to take multiple choice tests; that's one of the big not-so-secret secrets of the SAT. Over the years, I've tried to pull together several approaches as I've counseled students. Most students can use their own experience and common sense to make this model work for them. For multiple choice tests, I tell students to take the following steps:

a. Cover the answer choices;
b. Read the question for meaning (i.e., not word by word);
c. Read the question a second time for specific words or terms (e.g., "not," "always," etc.);
d. Try to think of an answer;
e. Uncover the answer choices;
f. Read each one;
g. If the answer you think of is among the answer choices, it's likely to be correct;
h. If that answer isn't there, consider the answers provided and notice if any seem correct;
i. If not, cross out any answers that are clearly incorrect;
j. Mark questions that you don't complete and move on to the next one;
k. Work through all questions this way;
l. Now go back to the questions you have not yet completed;
m. Reconsider the answer options and look for answers that jump out as being correct;
n. If there is no clear answer, try to eliminate any other incorrect answers;
o. Move on one more time;

p. When coming back a third time, see if something jumps out;

q. If not, guess.

## 4. Tips for essay questions

Being prepared for essay questions involves knowing the instructor or professor. Are there certain themes, topics or even pet peeves that tend to come up in class regularly? In many cases, professors pretty much tell students what the essay questions will cover. It's not unusual for professors to give a list of potential essay questions. More often than not, it's not terribly difficult to figure out what to expect with essay questions.

A problem that many students run into with essay questions is that they don't write enough, or at least not enough of the right stuff. The two most common comments on essay questions are "expand" and "elaborate." But what does this mean?

Many students think that they just need to give a basic answer or state their opinions on essay questions. As far as all that other detail stuff, well the professor knows what the student is talking about and knows that student knows it, right? Wrong.

First, the purpose of a test is for you to *demonstrate* what you know, not for the professor to *assume* what you know. Students need to provide extensive details and facts. It's much better to err on the side of too much information, as long as the "too much" is relevant.

Second, the question may ask for an opinion, but opinions need to be supported. Just because there are no right or wrong answers does not mean that all essays are created equal. Some arguments are better than others, including those with logical support of specific evidence.

Finally, think examples. A major point in an essay should always be supported by examples, usually the more specific and detailed the better. A standard way to study for essay tests is to guess/brainstorm possible questions and then memorize supporting examples or information for each one. Savvy students realize that certain information can be incorporated into answers for practically any question, and they make sure to come to the test loaded with generic facts and details.

Another good survival skill is to recognize the professor's opinions on topics. Generally, it's safer to align your opinions with those of the professor on a test; class is a much better and safer time to challenge a professor's position. For those students who just have to take the counter argument on a test — do it well! And don't get suckered into thinking that professors are trying to brain-wash students. It's probably a healthier approach to accept that professors are trying to see if students understand their opinions or theories. It's up to the student whether to side with them or not.

## 5. Avoid careless errors

Careless errors occur in direct proportion to lack of preparation. Students who are well prepared are calm, cool, and collected and tend not to make a lot of careless mistakes. Unprepared students are usually in a panic — exactly the state of mind that leads to carelessness.

Here are a few tips for avoiding careless errors:

a. Begin by looking over the entire test. There are countless horror stories of students who never turned over the last page of a test to discover there were still more questions!

b. Avoid reading a question incoreectly. As with multiple choice questions, I suggest that students read through all questions a first time for overall meaning and then reread them word by word to make sure that they have not missed an essential qualifier (e.g., "not," "always," "except," etc.).

c. Use time and content management strategies. It's better to rush through a section that has relatively little point value than one with major point value, so tackle big-ticket questions first. Looking over the whole test at the beginning helps with laying out a plan.

d. After finishing, check the test over item by item to make sure that you haven't skipped or missed any questions.

e. If possible, go through all questions a second time looking for careless errors, such as penciling in the wrong bubble on a scantron or forgetting a critical qualifier (e.g., "not," "always," "except," etc.) in an essay.

f. Don't panic. Having a test-taking strategy helps students control anxiety and fear.

## 6. Using accommodations wisely

For the most part, this ought to be a no-brainer. Students who have accommodations for test taking need to use them. I've met with countless students with learning disabilities who have documented access to accommodations but fail to turn in the form to the professor. Even if you decide that an accommodation isn't necessary, it always makes sense to keep the option open. Using accommodations in college is another example of self-advocacy because it's your responsibility to communicate with the instructor.

Although extended time is the most common test-taking accommodation, it is not the magic remedy for all test-taking woes. To begin with, students who don't know the material will not do better with extended time; they only have more time to show what they don't know. I've also seen students fritter away extra time. They seem to think that they can take as many breaks as they want, they don't focus, and then they are shocked when even the extra time runs out. I remember one student who used much of his extended time to take cigarette breaks. His extra time literally went up in smoke! Extended time is a great accommodation, but you still need to use time management and test-taking strategies.

Administering tests in an alternate location is another frequent test accommodation. It makes a lot of sense to get students with learning disabilities out of distractible environments. However, this may mean taking the test apart from the instructor, who is usually the best resource during the test itself. Be sure to weigh the pros and cons of leaving the classroom to take tests. If possible, I recommend taking the est in the professor's office or a nearby space so that the student may stay in contact with the instructor.

## Writing Papers

### 1. Macro-organizing and scheduling

When I was a senior in college, I had to write a 100-plus page thesis. At my alma mater, the senior thesis takes on mythic proportions, creating a mounting sense of shock and awe from freshman year until the beginning of senior year, when full-fledged panic sets in. Somehow, I managed to complete most of my research and the first of five chapters of my thesis before the spring semester. When I returned to school after winter break, I immediately had trouble getting to sleep at night. I realized I had about eighty pages left to write, and the clock was ticking.... loudly. While I tossed and turned in my bed, visions of 80 danced in my head. How could I ever manage such a monumental task? I still feel anxiety simply from remembering how panicked I felt. Talk about feeling like things were out of control!

When I had about two months (eight weeks) to get this thing done I figured if I could write ten pages per week, I'd make it. Ten pages a week didn't sound great, but at least it sounded manageable. I'd written ten page papers before, certainly in less than a week, and I could do it again. I did one more calculation. Ten pages a week is two pages per day for five days. Somehow, writing two pages a day seemed less daunting than ten pages per week.

In order to keep myself focused, and because it gave me a much better sense of control, I drew up a "jailhouse calendar." I marked daily deadlines and page goals for the next eight weeks. I generally mapped out two pages to write on any given day; occasionally I might have shot for three. I gave myself two days off per week. The plan was simple. I would not leave the library until I had met each day's quota. When I did, I crossed out that day and deadline on the calendar (the "jailhouse" part).

The days turned to weeks, the weeks to months, and the due date right after spring break loomed. For many students, the senior thesis was an inexorable march through procrastination, panic, denial, hiding, and finally surrender to full-blown crisis mode. (I won't comment on the role beer played in all this.) On the other hand, I was able to count down the time with a sense of confidence—most of the time! The physical act of crossing out page deadlines on my calendar gave me a reassuring sense that I would finish the assignment.

Creating a jailhouse calendar works for almost any kind of writing task. The student begins by notating not only the due date, but the number of pages required as well. It just takes simple math to figure out how many days of writing it will take to reach the requirement based on quotas of two to three pages per day. However, many papers involve research, and all require planning and pre-writing/outlining before actually writing the paper, and revising (editing and rewriting) after the first draft is completed. Students need to plan out time for these components of writing.

As an example, let's take a look at the steps for writing a fifteen-page paper over the course of three weeks.

    a. Week one starts with selecting a topic. Plan out several or more hours this first week to conduct preliminary research, look at possibilities, and decide on the topic. Interesting topics are easier to write about than boring ones, so choose an interesting topic to the extent that you have a choice.

    b. Plan out the hours you will need to examine the primary research and take notes.

    c. By the beginning of week two, you should be ready to write the outline for the paper.

    d. With ten days left, start writing at a pace of two to three pages per day.

    e. You should be able to finish a few days ahead of schedule, have someone (ideally the instructor) look the paper over, and revise as necessary.

    f. Finally, turn in a clean final copy on the due date.

## 2. Communicating with the instructor

As the person who reads and evaluates a paper, the instructor is the only one who knows the secrets to a good paper—at least for this class. Students should not assume they understand what an instructor wants in a paper.

Before starting to write, you need to check in with the professor, especially regarding topic and format. You also need to check in with the professor during the writing process. Email makes it possible to share work instantly. It's a good idea to get feedback from the professor after writing the first few pages. Of course, you have to judge the instructor's temperment. Some instructors are pleased to look at a paper in progress multiple times; others are not. Even instructors who are not overly helpful in the writing process are usually willing to give feedback on an entire paper if you can turn it in before the deadline. In many cases, it's worthwhile to negotiate an earlier deadline in order to get comments and reactions before handing in the final product.

Finally, it's important for you to speak with instructors after getting your paper back. I cannot tell you how many times students will tell me that they don't understand why they received a certain grade for a paper. "Talk to your professor," I say. "But it's too late now," the student counters. "Not if you want to figure out how to do better next time," I reply. Figuring stuff out in college isn't rocket science (unless you're at M.I.T.), but it does take communication and self-advocacy.

In addition to the professor, many other sources may provide useful feedback. Students often forget that they are writing for an audience—the reader. While the professor is the primary audience, teaching assistants, other students in the class, students who have previously taken the class, advisors, even residential advisors or roommates may be enlisted in the writing process. Always get a second opinion.

## 3. Avoid the blank page syndrome

Back in the old days, before starting to write a paper, I'd spread out my research and note cards and then stare at a blank piece of paper. I'd wait for a moment of inspiration... and wait, until I seemed to have some cogent thought. I'd scribble it down, look at it, decide it wasn't working, ball up the paper, throw it away, and start staring at the next blank piece of paper. There was something about that blank piece of paper. It stared back at me, mocking me, taunting me that I'd never be able to get down anything worthwhile.

As I moved from No. 2 pencils to word processing, I discovered a whole new approach to writing. Now, whatever the writing project, I start writing immediately so that I never have a blank page staring back at me. For example, when I conduct research for a paper, as I select an article to use, I immediately open up my Word folder and type in the reference information. Done! One of the entries that I'll need to have in the references section is already there. As I start to read or skim the article, I copy the reference entry into a new page and write down any notes. By the time I've looked at three or four articles, I have a good start on the references section plus a few pages of notes.

As I do this type of preliminary writing, I think about what my paper will be like and try to picture where each note will fit. I might start building sections by cutting and pasting. Usually, I like to have a thorough outline. Then, as I write notes, I often can immediately plug them into the appropriate section of the paper. Before I have even given much thought to how to start writing the paper, I am writing it. I don't wad up my writing into a ball and throw it away if I don't like it. Instead, I clip it and paste it in the back of the document. What sounds crummy today may be just the ticket when I look at the paper tomorrow. By immediately writing down whatever might work, I avoid the blank page syndrome. My work isn't yet done, but I have a much greater sense of confidence and control.

## 4. Organize, reorganize, and edit

Remember that part about balling up the piece of paper and throwing it out? I can recall several scenes of dorm rooms covered in wadded up paper balls, often with a blank page sitting in the typewriter. The problem was that if you wrote something and were not sure where it would fit or if it sounded right, there wasn't much you could do. Rewriting on the same page was too messy and reorganizing was virtually impossible without starting over again.

Word processing has made organization, reorganization, and revision relatively simple processes. Nothing has to be thrown away. A writer can rewrite and revise in the middle of a sentence or paragraph. The final draft of a paper used to be a really big deal. Back in the day, once you had the final draft, that was it. A change here, a change there, and all of a sudden you'd either have a mess of smudged White-Out or you'd have to type the whole paper over again. Today, with word processing, changes may be made at any time, and the copy will always look clean. Organizing and reorganizing are important components of editing and are often overlooked by many students. Editing means rereading what you have written — over and over. It means critically asking the question, "Will the reader understand what I am saying?" It means thinking about and then deciding on the best logical flow — for a sentence, a paragraph, a section, and the entire paper.

For example, after I write a sentence, I look at it again to see if I have phrased it well. Are some words unnecessary? Do I need something more? Is the meaning clear? As I look over paragraphs, I often decide to cut, paste, and reorder sentences to create a better logical flow. I also examine transitions, especially between paragraphs, sometimes discovering that it makes sense to end one paragraph with a sentence that connects it to the next. I'll also reorder entire paragraphs, sections, and chapters. Thanks to word processors, the mechanics are easy. The thinking is not.

No matter what, there is never a bad decision. The "Undo Edit" button can always be hit! If I delete text that I no longer plan to use, I will paste it in the back of the document — just in case. I frequently save multiple versions of a paper. Students must not to be content with their first version of a paper. An extra half hour to an hour spent on reorganizing and editing will almost certainly raise the grade by a letter.

### 5. Use resources and accommodations

Virtually all colleges and universities offer resources to help students with writing. Most of the resources are available to all students, the most common of which is a writing lab. Writing labs almost always have writing tutors, who may be able to help you with steps from brainstorming a topic all the way to copyediting your completed paper.

Assistive technologies, ranging from organizational tools such as *Inspiration* (an organizational and outlining program for writing papers) to voice recognition software such as *Dragon Dictate*, may provide the exact assistance you need. Although specific accommodations for writing papers are less common, if you are entitled to them you should use them. These may include working with a tutor in the DS office (similar to a writing lab experience) or using a scribe.

## The Age of Assistive Technology

Everyday, new technology is introduced that can assist with organization. Devices such as the PDA and BlackBerry feature multifunction calendars and scheduling programs and store information for up to hundreds of contacts. In addition, email and the web are literally in the palm of your hand. However, communication technologies may be a huge distraction, especially for students who are easily distractible. The other day, I estimated that one out of every three students I saw walking around campus was talking on a cell phone. Add in other types of messaging, access to the web, and gaming, and these technological marvels of organization become the undoing of time management.

Love it or hate it—and most students love it—technology is here to stay. When history reviews the current epoch, I believe the technological revolution will be the defining characteristic. Virtually all students today have access to all sorts of technology. Technology is also indispensable to college life, particularly for teaching and learning. A number of colleges require all entering students to have laptops. A great deal of coursework is now computer or internet dependent, and using laptops in the classroom is becoming the norm.

Students with learning disabilities may use a variety of technologies. In many cases, assistive technology (AT) provides the best way to meet specific needs. The term, assistive technology, may conjure up images ranging from hearing aids to artificial intelligence, but the concept is relatively simple, and not necessarily hi-tech. The Assistive Technology Act of 1998 defines AT as "…. products, devices or equipment, whether acquired commercially, modified or customized, that are used to maintain, increase or improve the functional capabilities of individuals with disabilities…." In other words, AT is anything that helps students with learning disabilities make it in college. AT can be incredibly lo-tech. I worked with a student (not LD) who had hurt her back and could not sit down comfortably. I arranged to have an extra lectern or podium in place in her classrooms so that she could take notes standing up. That was AT—pretty basic, but still AT.

Information about AT abounds. The Alliance for Technology Access (http://www.ataccess.org/) is a good place to find general information. *LD OnLine*, a highly respected website on learning disabilities, offers a more specific focus on AT for students with learning disabilities (http://www.LDonline.org/LD_indepth/technology/technology.html), as does a site sponsored by the Learning Disabilities Association (LDA) (http://www.gatfl.org/ldguide/default. htm). Rather than try to provide a comprehensive overview of AT, I will share some observations about AT commonly used by students with learning disabilities.

### Tape recorder

Don't underestimate the power of the lowly tape recorder. Students should use a tape recorder with a counter so that they can write down the counter number during any part of a lecture that seems especially important. By doing so, they won't need to listen to the entire tape when they review, but rather can fast-forward to the important parts. Tape recorders are also great for organization and writing. Some people dictate notes to themselves using a tape recorder—from "Here's where the car is parked," to "Pick up pizza for dinner." Additionally, one of the best ways for some students to start a writing project is to "talk it out," which is the perfect use of a tape recorder. Say a few words into a tape recorder, type them down, and voila—no blank page. A number of famous writers hardly write at all. They dictate. It works.

### Kurzweil

I try to stay away from specific endorsements, but in the area of text to speech technology, nobody does it better than Kurzweil. Heck, Stevie Wonder was willing to pay more than a hundred grand twenty-five years ago to get the first Kurzweil reader. As of 2006, the Kurzweil 3000 is the latest generation of the product, which has evolved from a machine about the size of a small spaceship to a flatbed scanner and software. Many institutions have Kurzweil systems where the scanner lives in a central area but the software is available on a number of other computers; students may even purchase the software without the scanner for a more modest fee. Print material is scanned at the central area then downloaded to a CD or portable memory device, which can then be used on any computer with the Kurzweil software. Learn more at http://www.kurzweiledu.com/.

### Books on tape

Don't forget about RFB&D (Reading Foundation for the Blind and Dyslexic), as explained on page 66.

### Voice recognition systems

The best known software for translating spoken word into text is *Dragon Naturally Speaking,* formerly known as *Dragon Dictate* (http://www.dragonsys.ca). Other similar products are available. The user speaks into a microphone on the computer, and the speech appears immediately as text in a word format. Some versions have portable recording units for class lectures. The student records the lecture and later downloads to a PC where it appears as text. In my experience, these products require significant set-up work in order for the software to learn the user's voice. Even after repeated "training," the text may show up garbled. The fact that such programs are not routinely used by students probably attests to these kinks; however, this technology potentially offers wondrous advantages for many students with learning disabilities for whom writing is difficult. My bet is that the quality will improve.

### Software for developing ideas and organizing thinking

Many different products are available for helping students develop ideas and organize thinking. Students I know have been pleased with the program, *Inspiration*, which, among other things, allows the user to map out ideas for writing a paper in a variety of visual formats (Venn diagram, web, etc.) and creates outlines. It's a useful way to fight blank page syndrome as it encourages free and open-ended thinking/brainstorming. More information on *Inspiration* is available at http://www.inspiration.com/index.cfm.

ભ

# Tips for Students

## *Stand Up for Your Right(s)*

When you leave high school and get to college, everything changes. You have rights, but you don't have entitlements. When you were in high school, you didn't really have a choice about being identified as a student with learning disabilities. The school was responsible for identifying you as a student with a specific educational diagnosis and label, for providing all necessary testing and an IEP, and for ensuring that you received the special education services specified in your IEP. You were a special education student, like it or not. Once you leave high school, you don't have to tell anyone that you're a student with learning disabilities. But as you already know, I think it's a good idea to identify yourself, at least to those who can help you.

Disclosing early on may help you connect with DS. As I said earlier, it's important to assess the quality and goodness-of-fit of services at institutions that you are considering. Particularly at smaller colleges, letting the admissions program know that you have learning disabilities may be your passport to meeting with disability support service staff before you have to make a decision about attending. Increasingly, college programs for students with learning disabilities offer summer orientation programs. Being connected from the start tends to facilitate a good line of communication.

If you did not inform the admissions program of your learning disabilities, you will have to face disclosure issues once you land on campus. In fact, even if you self-identify during the admissions process, it is not guaranteed that anything will come of this disclosure unless you make a request. Again, you may decide that you're going to put your learning disabilities behind you and make a clean break. You might be pretty darned tired of having the LD label dogging you wherever you go. I understand your feelings, but think through what it will take for you to be successful in college.

By disclosing your learning disabilities, you'll be better off. You'll have some sort of support system, and you can be the boss in deciding who should and shouldn't know about your disabilities. Connect with the institution's DS as soon as possible and provide the requested documentation. You decide who, if anyone, is allowed to access this information. Even if you allow access, you can control who sees this information and who does not. You also have the right to access your records and may withdraw them at any time.

So you've found DS. You're at the door or on the phone. What do you do now? Introduce yourself. Identify yourself as a student with learning disabilities. See if you may talk with someone now or if you should make an ap-pointment. Ask to see a staff member who is a learning disabilities specialist. Remember, you're in college now. Don't be shy. You have to take care of yourself. Of course, after reading this book, you'll have already done your self-study and have become a pro in terms of knowing your strengths, weaknesses, and needs! Seriously, the more that you know about yourself, your evaluation reports, and your IEPs, the better able you'll be to initiate a dialogue about what will help you in college.

## *Understanding Your Learning Disabilities*

To more thoroughly and clearly understand your individual learning strengths and weaknesses, I suggest reviewing your psychological evaluations with a staff member from your college's the LD support program who can help you wade through the swamp of technical information and decipher the meaning behind all those tests and scores. To provide some context for examining your evaluations and to provide a systematic method, I encourage you to follow these steps:

1. See if you can remember what was going on in your life before you went for an evaluation (e.g., poor grades; difficulties in school or home; retained in a grade; tutoring; anxiety, frustration, confusion, etc.). Had this been going on for awhile? How old were you?

2. Interview your parents about this period in your life. Why did they have you evaluated? What were their specific concerns? Did the school/teacher suggest it? Why?

3. What do you remember about meeting with the person who conducted your evaluation? What kind of tests did you take (not the names, but the types

of things you actually had to do)? How did you feel (scared, didn't care, pleased, etc.)?

4. What do you remember about what happened after the evaluation came back? Did you talk about it? Did anything change at school (e.g., did you wind up in a special class)? Did anything change at home?

Once you have answered the preceding questions, look at the evaluation report with a staff member from support services and take note of the following: What tests (provide names) were given? What were the results (scores on tests and subtests)? What do they mean? What were the conclusions and recommendations in the report? Do you agree with the evaluation report? Why or why not? What are your strengths? Be broad. Be creative. Talk to people you know well. Finally, write up your own analysis. I encourage you to make this paper free of technical terminology; rather, I hope that you will create a self-portrait that will be under-standable to someone not familiar with learning disabilities.

The examiner's commentary is usually the most useful piece of the evaluation. Good educational evaluators not only explain the results, meanings, and implications of every subtest, but they also attempt to synthesize all those results into a coherent whole. A review of this type of synthesis may help you to get beyond the numbers and identify clear strengths, weaknesses, and needs. Reviewing documentation and writing the "self-portrait" will help you develop a more specific knowledge of what your learning disabilities are and how these learning disabilities affect your educational experiences.

For the second project, you will apply this knowledge to reflect on how you have coped in the classroom. Again, I suggest following these steps:

1. Think about any classes in which you've had real difficulty. Why do you think you've had problems? How much of your difficulty do you think was related to your learning disabilities? How much was because of other reasons? Were you aware of these reasons at the time?

2. In what classes have you used specific compensations and/or accommodations? Were these helpful? Why or why not?

3. In what classes have you been most successful? To what do you attribute your success?

4. What have you learned about taking classes? In which courses are you most likely to be successful? In which might you have difficulty? Will this affect your course selection and how you approach these courses?

I take great satisfaction in reading students' stories of self-discovery and success. But what ultimately means the most to me is when students affirm that the exercises have been meaningful to them—an almost universal reaction. Here are comments from some of my students:

> • I am impressed with the whole experience of finding out about my learning disability. It makes me appreciate how much I have accomplished even though I was not learning the same way as the rest of my peers....To me, being successful means that you come out on

top with more knowledge of yourself than when you started.  — Alice

• At this time, I am not sure what the future holds in store for me, but I am confident in my abilities and believe that I will succeed. I've had to overcome so many obstacles in the past, so there is no reason for me to believe that I won't be able to accomplish my goals once again.  — Mick

• What I never understood while attending (high school) was how I learn best as a student with learning disabilities, what I'm good at academically, and what my strengths and weaknesses are. Now I have learned more about myself and how my LD affects my life. I know that I am not stupid or lazy; I just don't learn the same way as others do, and there is nothing wrong with being different.
— Melanie

So go ahead. Look at those evaluation reports. Discuss them with people who can interpret them. Consider how well they describe you. Try to put these ideas in the context of your own personal history and experience. Learn about yourself. You just might like what you see.

You've reviewed documentation, determined accommodations and services, and magically morphed into a full-fledged college student. Guess you don't need to deal with support services anymore...at least not until next semester. Actually, I hope this is the case for upperclass students, but I urge you to err on the side of caution in your first and perhaps second year. Checking in with DS on a regular basis just makes sense as you're trying to figure out how to deal with this brave new world.

As much as I encourage you to get to know and use DS, I also will offer a word of caution. Although you may need to depend on your support services, especially during your first few days, semester, year or years, your ultimate goal is autonomy and independence as a young adult. Standing up for your rights does not mean becoming overly dependent. Programs usually do some things for you such as provide the necessary paperwork to set up your accommodations and, occasionally, communicate directly with professors or administrators on your behalf. Don't try to get staff to do things for you that you can and should do for yourself. *You* should be talking to your professors about your learning style, what works best for you, and what accommodations you may need.

### *Keeping It Together*
If you follow my tips in the section called "Taking Control," you'll already have your Daily/Weekly Schedule, (Exhibit 2.4), practically filled up before the semester has even begun; but you've still only done the preliminaries. From this point on, you want to sketch out each week in some detail. Start by looking at what's due each week and when you should get it done. Do this for all your requirements. The Progress in Courses chart, (Exhibit 2.3), will help, especially because you already will have papers, tests,

and projects written down. Consequently, you should have a more realistic sense of how and where you will find the time to keep up with all your other assignments, particularly readings.

You need to figure out how and where you'll prepare for tests, papers, or projects. For big projects and term papers, you will often need to map out several weeks of preparation. In this case, you should break down the project into weekly goals or chunks. At the end of each week, write down your goal. In this way, you will know what you should get done each week. As each week comes up, plan more specifically. Allocate days and times for reaching that week's goal.

The more you use your planner, the more useful it will be to you. Use it for both long-term and short-term planning. Generally, if you sit down with it once per week to do short-term planning for that week and once to catch up on or add long-term goals or events, you will be in good shape. You will still need to use it every day, but at this point most of what you write will be crossing off things that you have accomplished. That's a good feeling.

### Want Pizza and Beer? Get a Job

Loans can get you through the four or five years of being a full-time undergraduate. Your increased earning power as a college graduate will more than cover this amount over a period of time. Remember that most doctors and lawyers had to take out even bigger loans for their professional training. They seem to have been able to pay off their loans with more than a little left to spare.

Nevertheless, you should think about what it means to take on possibly sizable debt. You will have to repay the money, a process that takes a number of years. Especially as you're starting out in a new career, you may find that your monthly loan payment takes a big chunk out of your meager paycheck. Some individuals wind up defaulting on their loans. It seems like a quick fix, but it will mark you for life, making credit difficult to obtain. That could result in serious difficulty buying a house, car, or even financing your children's education. So if you take out big loans to go to college (and many, many students do), be aware of what you're getting into.

In addition to tuition (and room and board if you live away from home), you'll have to buy books every semester. It may not seem like a big deal until you realize that, on average, college students today spend around $500 on books each semester. That's $1,000 per year or $4,000 over four years. Your expenses don't stop there. You may have lab fees. You may need to buy a computer. Do you want to look good, perhaps make sure that you have your official college sweatshirt (or ten)? It's not free. Are you thinking about joining a sorority or fraternity? Have you considered initiation fees and dues? Do you like to have fun—go out, play video games, listen to CDs, etc? Oh, and maybe you've heard that some college students like to party and drink (not an official recommendation of this book!). Who's going to pay for your good times? Daddy's money? Maybe, maybe not.

So what do you do? Get a job. For many college students, summers devoted to having fun and spending whatever pocket money is available are luxuries of the past.

In fact, many college-bound high school students start saving money through summer employment early in their high school careers. Many teens also have part-time jobs during the school year.

For many students and their families, part of the financial plan to pay for college involves more than summer employment. You may need to plan to work while you're in college. In fact, according to the third annual Alloy College Explorer Study, 78% of college students have some kind of job. Increasingly, working to put yourself through school is becoming the norm.

You will find many part-time employment opportunities in college. In most colleges and universities, students who receive financial aid are eligible for college work-study employment. Most schools can virtually guarantee employment to students on financial aid; some institutions may require employment as part of the financial aid package. If you don't receive financial aid (or don't automatically qualify for work-study), you can still find employment opportunities, from working for different types of college services and departments, to temporarily helping out with different events. Usually, you'll be able to find a campus employment office that will post all sorts of employment opportunities. In some places, student agencies hire students for everything from tutoring to typing, from pushing a hot dog cart (I was once the "Weenie Man" at college) to pushing alumni to give money, from bartending to babysitting. And in the typical college town, there is a virtual industry that depends on student labor. It's not particularly glamorous work—delivering pizza, waiting or bussing tables, and so on—but you can find the types of jobs that work with your schedule. Another

industry that works well for part-timers with erratic schedules is telemarketing (if you can deal with irate callers
screaming at you). Some students find an unanticipated
benefit from their part-time work: They actually learn a
marketable skill. The bottom line is that there is work to be
found if you look for it.

Students with learning disabilities need to consider
additional issues that may affect their choice of work, or
whether they even work at all. During freshman orientation
at my college, I tell students with learning disabilities that
they will have to work harder than other students if they are
to be successful. It may not seem fair, I tell them, but it's the
reality that successful students with learning disabilities have
to face. So before you sign on as the night cook at the 24-
hour greasy spoon, you'd better determine if you have
available time to work.

The keys to holding a part-time job while being a
successful student—organization, time management, and
prioritizing—should already be familiar to you. Before picking up a job, you need to know how much time per week
you really have available. Start by adding up your hours of
class each week with the total amount of study time that you
have estimated with the Goal Planning Program (Exhibit
2.2). Add in the time for any other routines such as athletics,
working out, and extra curricular activities. Subtract this
number from seventy. What is left is the amount of time per
week you can reasonably devote to a part-time job, assuming that you're willing to use all seven days of the week
efficiently.

I've seen an increasing number of students, with and without learning disabilities, dig themselves into deep holes academically because they spend too much time working to make money. Some of these students say they simply don't have a choice; it's the only way to pay the bills. As much as I understand this and actually admire such determination, I tell them that they do have a choice, and, in fact, they have made a bad one. Killing yourself to pay for your tuition does not accomplish anything if you're not passing courses or if you're putting yourself at risk of not being able to graduate.

Don't put yourself in this position. And if you do find yourself in this position, reevaluate. Instead of working your way through college, you may need to put that dream on hold while you work full-time, minimize your expenses, and save, save, save. Or, you might be better off being a part-time student rather than a full-time one. Of course, there are undoubtedly other ways to reorganize your finances, but you must consider your priorities. Your priority should be your success as a student. You already face more challenges than most other students do. You cannot afford to stack the deck against yourself. You must be realistic about the time you can devote to working without it interfering with your studies.

Occasionally, I see students working too much because they like having extra money. They soon develop a lifestyle that makes them think they cannot afford to work any less than they already do. I've been working with a student whose grades have been falling steadily for the last couple of semesters. His academic demise correlates with his spending about forty hours per week at two part-time jobs.

In my mind, he doesn't really need all that money. But he now has a credit card and a credit line, and he has managed to put together a lifestyle that is landing him in some major debt. He just bought a $10,000 motorcycle, virtually assuring him of the need to come up with another sizable chunk of cash each month. Again, the issue is setting priorities. The problem is that most students in this situation don't realize that they have made bad choices. They have not stayed focused on priorities. They have not assessed the long-range implications of their actions.

While avoiding impulsive temptation and seeing beyond the moment are difficult for many college students, students with learning disabilities need to be especially careful in weighing their priorities. After all, impulsiveness, difficulty understanding cause and effect relations, and problems with predicting long term consequences are characteristics of learning disabilities for some individuals. If you feel that you share some of these traits, use extra caution and disciplined thinking in picking up part-time work.

Some students work too many hours because they get sucked in by the demands of their part-time jobs: "Sheila called in sick. Can you pick up another shift today and tomorrow?" Or, "Hey, this is the busy season. We're going to need some extra hours from you." The pressure may be real or imagined. It's hard to say no, especially when it's your boss. Once again, remember your priorities. No part-time job is worth jeopardizing your academic success.

I'm not trying to scare you out of working. In fact, I think a part-time job is a great part of the college experience. Remember, I was once the Weenie Man. Having a job may help you improve your time management, organization, and prioritization. Being very busy almost forces this.

Having a job may also help students with learning disabilities improve and develop adaptive skills and coping strategies. Having a job puts you in the real world where you have to fend for yourself. If at all possible, you should try to find work that in some way resembles what you think you'll be doing after college. This is a chance to experiment a little, to see what works well for you and what does not, to try out self-advocacy skills, to show just how competent (and creative) you can be.

## Tips for Parents

### Flying the Helicopter

Remember Alice, who was willing to lay her struggles with depression on the table? At a follow-up meeting, Alice made another good decision. She brought along her parents. At the conclusion, the psychologist told them, "To be honest, you are the only parents who have ever called to make an appointment with me to find out exactly what is going on with their kid. I am very impressed with how your family is so close that Alice would want to share this information with you." To Alice, it was only natural to include her parents in her search for self-discovery. After all, they had witnessed her struggles and had always been there to support her. Sometimes, self-discovery and understanding is a group effort. Sharing and caring can provide great dividends.

Don't expect that all faculty and administrators at college will welcome your involvement with open arms. Many feel that parents' heavy involvement in their childrens' lives causes all sorts of problems. Few terms elicit more knee-jerk reactions with faculty than "helicopter parents," those parents that are continually hovering over their children. It's like waving a red flag at a bull. It's getting so bad that President Rebecca Chopp of Colgate University has declared war on helicopter parents, or at least is trying to keep them grounded. Colgate used to give parents a sheet of administrators' phone numbers. Now, parents get a statement about Colgate's philosophy of self-reliance, and they may even be asked to do summer reading on how to let go. Other schools are taking a similar approach, even going so far as having "parent bouncers," students who are paid to discourage parents from butting in on the day-to-day activities of their children.

You probably will not be physically thrown off your child's campus, but you might want to consider showing a little restraint. Instead of calling your kids, why not wait for them to call you when they want to talk. Alice's parents did not hover around her, constantly making the first move. They waited for Alice to call them. Alice made the decision to bring them to the meeting, not the other way around. Your child will likely hit a few bumps in the road the first year, and the first semester in particular. If there is a problem, most students will call home.

If you decide to contact the college to see how your child is doing, you may be shocked to discover that professors and administrators will tell you virtually nothing. They can't, because your child's right to privacy is protected under the Family Educational Rights and Privacy Act (FERPA). Your child may sign a waiver giving you permission to access certain kinds of information. However, I suggest you allow your child the autonomy that FERPA provides and instead work on fostering an open, honest, and increasingly adult relationship.

Developing and maintaining a relationship with someone at the DS office may wind up providing a safe harbor when your child hits those stormy waters of college life. I cannot begin to describe the panic that sets in for many freshmen when they hit their first set of midterms, or when those first big papers come due. Students with learning disabilities are even more likely to feel positively overwhelmed. They may find some solace in seeing that most of their buddies are similarly freaked out, but they need assurance, they need answers, they need to know what to do. Binge drinking will not solve the problems, although it's a common coping strategy. For students who have built a relationship with DS, or even for those who haven't, the DS office is a place to go where people will not only understand what it's like to be a freshman, they will be fine-tuned to deal with the more specific issues of students with learning disabilities.

You may have heard that what happens to students during their first six weeks of college has the most impact on whether they will stay or leave. Administrators often take this as gospel, and more than one first-year program places the greatest emphasis on the first six weeks of college. Here's something that most of those talking heads don't tell you: virtually no research supports the "first six weeks" phenomenon. So when you get that hysterical "Take me home" call several weeks into the first semester, take a deep breath, and help your child to hang on, not to let go. First-year students are probably dealing with the toughest transition they've had to make so far in their lives, but that's what they're in school to learn to do. Support your child's struggle to grow up. Don't enable your child to give up. On more than one occasion, I've given students some basic old-school advice: "Suck it up." Their parents have thanked me.

### Paying for Assistive Technology — Hi Tech at Lo Cost

I strongly recommend that college students, particularly those with learning disabilities, go to college equipped with a laptop. Laptop prices have moved below the $500 mark, roughly the same amount as for books for one semester. A student should get more use out of a laptop than any other piece of technology (although video games and cell phones offer stiff competition).

I've promoted the use of the tape recorder. Here's another plus — it's cheap. For thirty bucks, your child can have a tool that will have multiple uses over four years. It probably will never need an upgrade!

I don't mean to take the wind out of the sails of the technological revolution, but two of the best assistive technologies for students with learning disabilities are paper and pencil. The most useful and used assistive technology tools that I employ are goal planning and daily schedule sheets. Bells and whistles are not always necessary to help students with learning disabilities.

### *Mom, Dad — Send Money*

We might convince ourselves that when we were kids, we didn't expect our parents to be cash cows. That probably ranks right up there with the myth of walking to school five miles uphill each way, respecting our elders without question, never getting into trouble, or abstaining from sex, drugs, and rock n' roll. If you were a child of the '60s or the '70s... come on. As the saying goes, if you can remember the '60s, you weren't there. The revisionist history we unload on our kids is a topic for another book, but when I think back on my misspent youth, I get a different picture. Starting at some point in high school, it seemed as if whenever I walked up to my father and said, "Hey, dad..." he'd cut me off with, "OK. How much?" After all, when you're a teen, you need cash. Are our kids bigger consumers then we were? Maybe. But we are also the ones who have ratcheted up the lust of materialism. It should not be surprising that our children "need" tons of stuff.

Before your child begins college, you need to sit down and discuss what you will pay for and what you will not. Estimate the expenses for the semester that you are willing to finance. It's usually preferable to put the amount in a debit card account for your child, but some caution is warranted. If your child has not had much experience or responsibility with managing money, the account could be dry before textbooks have been purchased. In many cases, parents need to put together a transition plan. For example, in the first semester or so, mom and dad pay directly for the essentials (textbooks, materials, etc.) and the student controls a smaller account for non-essentials. As time goes on, the student becomes more responsible for financial matters.

No matter your means, I suggest drawing the line somewhere. It's simply not good life training to lead your child to believe that money is always available for every whim. Your child can learn to live without or be responsible enough to pay for what he or she wants or needs.

Household budgets drive the lifestyle of the student. In some families, the student may be expected to be responsible for a host of costs, including tuition. If your child will need to work to meet expenses, you need to make sure the situation is reasonable. Ten to fifteen hours of work per week for a full-time student is fine (and even linked to higher graduation rates). Beyond that, you're playing with fire. If being a full-time student requires having a full-time job, it's not time to be a full-time student.

# Tips for Guidance Counselors

### Promoting Self-Advocacy in College

One of the best things you can do as a high school guidance counselor to prepare students with learning disabilities for college is to help them build and improve their self-advocacy skills. Many of your students with learning disabilities may not be ready to deal with a college DS office, much less professors and instructors, when they first get to college. You can help prepare these students for college by working with them to develop highly individualized strategies while allowing them to discuss their fears, anxieties, and perhaps some bad experiences that have made it difficult for them to talk to others about their learning disabilities.

DS offices in many colleges have specific programs to help students learn to communicate their needs. For example, in some programs, as students discuss accommodations with a DS staff member, that member will ask them how they will explain their needs and subsequent accommodations to the instructor in each course. By rehearsing, discussing, and fine-tuning strategies, students learn what to say to their professors, and how to say it. Guidance counselors in high school can offer this type of preparation as well; it does not require highly specialized training. Basic counseling skills, an appreciation of the student's strengths and weaknesses, and good ol' common sense can get the job done.

Similarly, group role-playing often helps students develop self-advocacy skills. In an informal support group that we offer students at my college, I sometimes put students through their paces by playing "good professor/bad professor." We set up a hypothetical but common situation, such as asking a professor for an extension on the due date for a paper. The "good" professor may be accommodating, but the "bad" professor is armed with an endless list of questions and rebuttals. The students learn it's better not to get into such a situation in the first place, but if they do, they need to be prepared, particularly in establishing their credibility.

They learn that a professor will be more likely to work with and accommodate a student who has clearly been making a determined effort throughout the semester (e.g., no class cuts, good class participation, completion of homework assignments, extra credit projects, etc.) than a student who has been largely AWOL until crunch time. Students also learn that how they present themselves makes a difference. They need to use effective social skills. Whining isn't one of them. Neither is lack of eye contact. Nor is it wise for students to ask for special consideration when clearly in the midst of a hangover. It may sound goofy, but looking like a professional young adult rather than a reject from *Animal House* creates a more favorable impression. The list goes on.

One of the most beneficial outcomes of role-playing comes from student-to-student interaction. Observing others dealing with familiar situations allows students to reflect on how they would handle a similar situation. Students often provide their peers with the best feedback and commentary because their responses have a ring of greater authenticity. Wonderful benefits may result from students sharing their experiences, talking about what they have done in similar situations, and explaining what has worked for them and what has not. Fellow students are often the best source for survival tips. After all, they've been there, done that. Having the opportunity to practice social and self-advocacy skills in "safe" environments, where they can make and learn from mistakes, observe others, and discuss and share strategies, provides students with a sound mechanism for building and improving self-advocacy skills.

### Translating Psychobabble

If you want to be a helpful resource for students with learning disabilities, you must be able to understand as well as help them understand their psychoeducational evaluations. Reports tend to have a great deal of psychological and educational jargon or psychobabble. Additionally, they are based on theoretical perspectives that may or may not be clearly explained. Part of the problem with trying to understand learning disabilities is that even professionals in the field don't agree on very much. Did you know that there are at least ten different definitions of learning disabilities that have achieved some level of prominence? The process of identifying learning disabilities based on a psychoeducational evaluation varies from state to state and sometimes from examiner to examiner.

Reviewing documentation does not provide magic answers or a quick fix. To begin with, a great deal of controversy exists about the testing used for determining learning disabilities. Most examiners are looking for a discrepancy between aptitude and achievement. That is, they usually give some type of IQ test, in most cases either the Woodcock-Johnson Test of Cognitive Ability or a Wechsler intelligence test, either the Wechsler Intelligence Scale for Children (WISC-III or IV) or the Wechsler Adult Intelligence Scale (WAIS). They compare the results of these tests with results from a battery of achievement tests such as the Woodcock Johnson Tests of Achievement or any of the tests listed in Exhibit 1.1 in Chapter One. While intelligence or aptitude tests measure potential for learning, achievement tests are designed to measure how much the student has actually learned. Generally, examiners will assess reading, writing, and math achievement, occasionally delving into other academic areas.

The diagnosis of learning disabilities depends, in large part, on whether a student's aptitude score is significantly higher than his score on at least one achievement test. This is what is known as the discrepancy between aptitude and achievement. It seems to explain the notion that people with learning disabilities have normal intelligence but have diffi-culty with learning in specific areas such as reading, writing or math. Occasionally, evaluations of college students and adults don't use achievement tests. Instead, the examiner looks for discrepancies within the subtests of the overall intelligence test. This theoretical perspective assumes that most individuals have similar scores from one subtest to the other. In contrast, persons with learning disabilities tend to have a great deal of scatter, scoring relatively well on some subtests and relatively poorly on others.

The list of reasons for the controversies about testing for learning disabilities is virtually endless. The new federal regulations for IDEA 2004 and the focus on Response to Intervention (RTI) will only serve to compound this issue. Do intelligence tests really measure one's intellectual poten-tial, or do they measure other things such as experience, culture, and so on? Are tasks on intelligence tests such as putting pictures in a logical sequential order, making analo-gies, or remembering strings of numbers backwards really the basis for what we call intelligence? What is intelligence? And even if, somehow, these are the tasks that define a person's intelligence, do they measure pure intelligence without, in some way, being affected by learning disabilities?

Achievement tests raise a similar slate of questions. Do these tests accurately measure what a person has learned? One of the main concerns about achievement tests is content validity. Some students go to schools where the curriculum matches the knowledge that is evaluated on a given achievement test. In this case, the test may have adequate content validity because the content of the test reflects the content to which the student has been exposed.

But suppose the curriculum content is vastly different from the content covered on the achievement test. Is this test measuring what the student has learned, or is it asking questions about content the student has never seen? It may accurately reflect that the student did not know the content of this test, but concluding that the student has been unable to learn the material (which is the presumption of the discrepancy approach) does not make much sense. Unless an achievement test reflects the curriculum the student has been taught, it does not measure what that student has actually learned or achieved. Consequently, the discrepancy between aptitude and so-called achievement may be meaningless.

Considering the possibility that test scores may not accurately reflect learning disabilities, you may wonder why you should even look at evaluations. First, it's important to know how the student scored on those tests, even if there are questions about validity. After all, administrators, teachers, other professionals, and sometimes parents have made decisions about the student based on those scores. Those scores are a piece of the student's history. Second, while arguments will always exist over how well we can test the psychological processes of cognition and learning, these tests do offer useful information. The tasks measured on IQ tests correspond to how we perform intellectual tasks in real life; and, in spite of the concerns over content validity in achievement tests, certain patterns are predictable. Students who score in the top or bottom ten percent on a given test will probably have relative strengths or weaknesses, respectively.

Look at test results with both eyes open and a lot of questions at the ready. Most importantly, go beyond the numbers. Evaluations are only as good as the examiner, and the explanations of the different tests will vary widely. Nevertheless, almost every examiner does provide narrative explanations. Usually, the examiner will describe what each subtest on an intelligence test is supposed to be measuring and what the score on each subtest consequently suggests. Similarly, the large areas of achievement tests (reading, writing, math) break down into smaller, more specific components or subtests. For example, reading usually includes both decoding and comprehension, which in turn include various components. Decoding may involve tests measuring phonics abilities, sight word recognition, and recognition by using context. Some tests may go even further, breaking down phonics, for example, into recognizing individual letter sounds, blends, beginning, middle, and ending sounds, etc. This level of specificity helps to pinpoint strengths and weaknesses in different areas of learning.

In general, be careful not to put too much emphasis on overall or composite scores. An "average" overall score does not mean much if the average is derived from very high scores on some subtests and very low scores on others. Look at the individual scores, and then read the examiner's interpretion of each of those scores.

### Paving the Way for Future Students

Routines are important. Most of us work more efficiently when we have some kind of structure, when our days have a predictability to them. College is probably the least structured environment that anyone ever encounters. In high school, unless they are breaking the rules, students are in class, study hall, or some sort of scheduled activity at any given time throughout the day. In the workforce, most people are expected to show up and leave at a certain time five days a week. They have a schedule. They have routines and expectations and not a lot of choices. They probably work at least forty hours per week.

In college or university, the only scheduled part of the week is classes. Total class time usually adds up to twelve to fifteen hours per week. That's college students' working week. And if they decide not to show up for a class, nothing seems to happen. No one docks their paycheck on Friday. The principal doesn't call their parents. But if they don't learn and apply time management and organizational techniques in college, they may graduate woefully under prepared for a competitive workforce.

You can help prepare college-bound students with learning disabilities for the challenge of setting and adhering to a schedule by working with them on time management skills in high school. Make sure they recognize the importance of sticking with a routine once they get into college. Remind them not to give up on the idea of keeping organized just because it may not work 100% of the time. It happens to everyone. No one is perfect. We all need to be cut some slack here and there.

The web offers some great opportunities for exploring and even having some fun with time management and organization techniques. For example, the Houghton-Mifflin website has a number of interactive features, notably from *Becoming a Master Student*, a widely used textbook that helps students develop effective time management approaches for college. (http://college.hmco.com/masterstudent/series/ becoming_a_master_student/11e/students/exercises/ index.html).

I particularly like the Interactive Time Chart presented on this site. It prompts students to input how many hours per week they spend in class, sleeping, studying, eating, working, exercise, fun, relationships, other. A student who uses the "2:1" rule for studying will be in good shape academically. You might point out that this well-prepared student can devote almost as much time to athletics or having fun as to studying.

When researchers at the University of Chicago studied students who were academically successful in college, they observed that these students had set routines and followed them. The students had schedules. They were very consistent about when, where, and what they studied. They not only developed some sort of daily schedule, they followed a routine for what they studied. For example, in a Monday afternoon two hour study block, the student does Statistics homework from 2:00-2:50 and reading for Religious Studies from 3:10 to 4:00. The student follows this routine every Monday. The student does not expect to get all the homework or reading done in the one block and schedules additional times as needed. Additionally, this student always studies in the same place.

There is no single best way to organize and plan. In fact, the best routines are the ones that are most personal. Establishing some type of routine to follow consistently is the key. As you know, college is as unstructured it gets. It takes a great deal of hard work to avoid being sucked into the chaotic lifestyle that many students in college embrace initially but then spend the rest of their years trying to change. The chaos of college is even more perilous for many students with learning disabilities. Students with learning disabilities often have difficulties with organization and planning. They don't need the same structure as other students; they need more. On top of this, some students with learning disabilities are more vulnerable to the temptations of a lifestyle where you make up the rules as you go along, or so it seems.

So many of the college students I know seem to have difficulty understanding the consequences of their behavior. They don't think that missing class, getting behind, partying whenever, etc. will affect them, at least until it's too late. They may then spend the rest of their time in school trying to dig themselves out of holes. And many of them, in spite of *knowing* better, manage to dig themselves back into those holes they say they're fighting so hard to get out of. Research tells us that many students with learning disabilities have more trouble than average students in terms of understanding consequences or cause and effect relationships. If Joe College doesn't get it that an out-of-control lifestyle leads to academic disaster, Joe College with learning disabilities may be even more in the dark.

Students with learning disabilities may be at greater risk of conforming to an irresponsible lifestyle. Although everyone wants to be part of the group, students with learning disabilities may be even more sensitive about wanting to fit in. In college, perhaps for the first time in their lives, they are fully part of the mainstream. They may think they should be able to party like everyone else. Encourage your students not to think this way. Other students will pressure them to get involved with partying, drinking, and irresponsible behavior. The consequences are bad for any student, but they may be disastrous for a student with learning disabilities. Part of being successful students with learning disabilities is the realization that the rules for them may be different: they have to work harder than most other students, they have to stay organized, they have to stay focused and disciplined.

Students will find themselves sorely tempted to cut classes, particularly large lectures where they are virtually anonymous. Class attendance is the strongest variable related to GPA. In order to do well, students need to know what the professor is really looking for, and nothing can replace going to class to find out this information. They have to be in class to get the syllabus and handouts. Still, not everything is on the syllabus. Sometimes, the professor may make a change or announce something new; if they're not there, they'll never know.

Maybe you remember some ugly scenes from your college days. The twenty page paper you didn't start until the night before it was due. Entire books that went unread. You missed so many classes that you couldn't understand the notes you borrowed just before the final exam. Perhaps you've had this dream: It's the day of the final exam, and you realize you've never attended the class. If just thinking about these scenarios raises your blood pressure, you have plenty of company. These college "nightmares" literally show up in people's sleep, often after they've been out of college for decades. College may be a lot of fun, but it can take you to the edge in terms of losing control.

For students with learning disabilities, losing control in college may lead to more than a few nightmares later in life. It might be the beginning of a tumble into a bottomless pit of frustration, distress, and even despair. The chances of dropping out (or being kicked out) of college rise exponentially for students with learning disabilities who don't have their organizational skills together. These individuals have a much greater chance of failing, being underemployed, and ultimately being dissatisfied.

### *Lurking on the Listserv*

As a guidance counselor, you probably know a lot about a few colleges, and a little about a lot of colleges. What do you know about disability services? Legal issues? What do you know about the types of problems that students with learning disabilities have with faculty and vice versa? What are disability service providers at individual colleges willing to do and not willing to do? You're only an email message away from the answers to your questions.

College and university disability service providers from schools throughout the country share their expertise on a listserv called the DSSHE-L (Disabled Student Services in Higher Education—Listserv). You may be able to join by sending a request to DSSHE-L@LISTSERV.ACSU.BUFFALO.EDU, or you might contact a DS staff member you know and ask him/her to forward your question to the list. By sending out your query to this association of professionals, you're likely

165

to receive a number of personal responses from experts in the field.

Joining the list has many advantages. You get to view tens if not hundreds of conversations everyday about current issues ranging from the sublime to the ridiculous. Reading the list regularly will give you a pretty good sense of what's going on with DS programs throughout the country. You get a sense of the hot button issues. You also get to see what pushes the buttons of DS professionals—not a bad insight when it comes time to deal with them. Finally, you may choose to get to know and interact with DS professionals through email correspondence, a networking opportunity that yields dividends for your students in the future.

**CHAPTER THREE**

**MAKING IT IN THE WORLD BEYOND**

## Is Grad School in the Future?

### It's Better the Second Time Around

When I started conducting research on successful adults with learning disabilities, I was surprised by how many of these individuals had gone to graduate school. Granted, grad school isn't the norm; in fact, plenty of highly successful individuals with learning disabilities have never even gone to college. However, for those who had gone on to grad school, what I found most intriguing was not that they had continued their education, but rather that almost all found grad school to be easier in some ways than any other part of their formal education. Elementary school was confusing. Middle and high school were times of teasing, frustration, and more confusion. In college, some things began to come together, but it was a bear to make it through the general education requirements, and every now and then a professor just seemed determined to make life miserable.

Grad school is different. Students with or without learning disabilities who move on to graduate education are going to school because they *really* want to. They are not merely interested in their field; they are passionate about it. And they ought to be good at it. In other words, grad school should represent goodness-of-fit, a situation in which students like what they study and are good at it.

Another reason that grad school seems to work for students with learning disabilities is the more personal and individual approach of most programs. Exceptions abound, of course, but many programs are relatively small. Students frequently have close relationships with professors, often being on a first-name basis. The student's major professor or advisor usually has only a handful of graduate students and tends to know them well. Although cut-throat competition exists in some programs, with faculty and staff pouring fuel on the fire, the majority of programs offer a supportive environment. In most programs, grad students have credibility because they were admitted; that is, they had to be good to get in. This type of atmosphere represents the kind of favorable social ecology that is so vital to adults with learning disabilities.

## LD Support Programs in Graduate and Professional Schools

By law, if a university offers services to undergraduate students with learning disabilities, the institution must offer the same services to graduate students. Consequently, any school that has a DS program provides support to graduate as well as undergraduate students. However, the experience of most graduate and professional program students tends to be different from that of undergraduates—and I should hope so!

I would expect a student with learning disabilities who has successfully graduated college with a record that meets graduate school admissions requirements to be quite independent. This does not mean that the student has no need for any support; rather, the student knows what kind of support is useful and is an effective self-advocate in ensuring he or she gets that support. Whereas the undergraduate years are a time to work on self-knowledge, self-actualization, and self-advocacy, the graduate years (and beyond) are the time to put these skills into practice. Old dogs can learn new tricks, and graduate students with learning disabilities may use the DS office to build their repertoire of strategies, but the office is no longer a home away from home. It's a professional service that students utilize in a professional manner.

The process of connecting with DS at the graduate or professional school level is the same as at the undergraduate level. Students need to identify themselves to the office and supply documentation of disability. Adult students have legal access to all of their educational records. It only makes sense for students to request copies of their complete undergraduate DS folders. The student may decide which of these records to pass on to the graduate DS office. It's possible that the graduate DS office will have a "recency" requirement regarding psychoeducational evaluations. However, if documented contact with an undergraduate DS program takes place, the school may waive the requirement of getting tested yet again.

## Consider This

Bob had a hard time in high school. From as early on as he could remember, he wanted to be a doctor. He was serious about his studies—dead serious—but nothing came easily, if at all. As a student with severe dyslexia almost fifty years ago, Bob struggled to eek out Cs, having to study seemingly forever to meet the minimum requirements. Meanwhile, his friends coasted their way to As and Bs. High school was a never-ending party for his peers, but Bob's teenage years were marked by long hours of slowly and painfully trying to contend with reading and writing.

Being a tenacious student, Bob was admitted to the state university. But he found college wasn't much different than high school. On the one hand, Bob had a chance to spend more time studying the sciences that he loved. On the other hand, the increased reading and writing demands, in addition to the demands of his science courses, made college an equally arduous trial. He knew he'd have to get top grades to get into medical school. He took the entire pre-med curriculum, and did alright, but not great, in his science and math classes. It was obvious he did not have the grades for medical school.

The poet, Langston Hughes, lamented that a dream deferred is the source of much sadness and regret. Bob realized that his hope of going to medical school might be deferred, but he would not give up on his quest to be a doctor. He would, however, have to reframe his dream. He decided to apply to dental school. There was a possibility he could get in. Just as importantly, he was able to come to see dentistry as a new calling. He realized that he could serve in the medical profession as a dentist and do pretty much all the things he had wanted to do as a medical doctor. For Bob, wanting to be a doctor was mainly about wanting to help people, and as any of us who've ever had dental problems can attest, a great dentist probably rates right up there with any other doctor we see.

So Bob applied to ten dental schools. He did not get into nine. It didn't matter. He got into one. It was his last choice, but that was not important. It was the path to his dream. The first part of dental school was hell. He had to read, read, read, and it hurt, hurt, hurt. Constantly battling his tendency to reverse words and letters, he found that after about ten minutes of reading slowly and painfully he would start to lose focus. He also discovered that if he tried to relax and clear his head for five minutes, he could go back to reading. He devised his own approach: ten minutes reading, five minutes off, over and over. He worked this way almost daily from eight at night until two in the morning. He wanted to give up, and if his wife had not pushed him, he might have.

Finally, the lecture classes were over and textbooks were a thing of the past. Instead of pushing pencils, Bob's class was now ready to get their hands dirty—or at least full of saliva. The students began their practical training, beginning with a dental mirror in one hand, a pick in the other, and a life-like model of the human head complete with working jaw and teeth. Bob remembers that most of the students were completely stumped trying to do intricate and delicate work through a mirror. It was as if their brains told their hands to do something, but their hands did the opposite. It was almost as if they had learning disabilities! But for Bob, this was a totally natural experience. He says that he had spent so much of his life seeing things in reverse that working with a mirror was a better fit! The world had straightened itself out. Bob had come home.

Bob did not give up on his dream, but he did have to reframe it. If he had not been willing to adapt to his circumstances, he may have lived out Langston Hughes's fear of a dream deferred. Bob's dream could have festered "like a sore" or stunk "like rotten meat." Instead, he took control and took care of himself. When life handed him lemons, he made lemonade. He redirected and advocated for himself. He seemed to find his true calling. Today, Bob's a great dentist. How do I know? He was my dentist, and I do place him on the same pedestal as any medical doctor.

Stanley Antonoff is another dentist—not just any dentist, but the former dean of the New York University School of Dentistry. He's also a dentist with learning disabilities. As the dean of the dental school, he noticed an apparently disproportionate number of dental students with learning disabilities. He developed a support program specifically for these students. Stanley speculates that some students with learning disabilities have a natural advantage in dentistry. He thinks that what happened to Bob isn't unusual—that some individuals who have dyslexic reversal problems find that life straightens itself out in the dental mirror.

# Self-Advocacy — The Gift That Keeps on Giving

## It's Never Too Late to Learn

I have been stressing the importance of self-advocacy throughout this book, particularly in college. In Chapter Two, I discussed the importance of deciphering psychoeducational evaluations, understanding what the law does and doesn't allow for, and using disability support services. Self-advocacy is where the rubber meets the road. Understanding one's strengths, weaknesses, needs, abilities, and personal style provides a great deal of personal satisfaction. This knowledge also has far wider implications, as it's the basis for effective self-advocacy. Self-advocacy is more than asking for or about accommodations and services; it's about asking for the specific accommodations and services that the individual needs, whether in the classroom or the workplace. In the world beyond college, a clear understanding of the American's with Disabilities Act (ADA) may become even more important.

How do people with learning disabilities become effective self-advocates in their lives beyond college? We all know some people who are natural self-advocates. They exude confidence; they stick up for themselves; they have no problem telling others what they want and need. In reality, most of us don't feel so self-assured. But we can learn how to take better care of ourselves. To begin, let's acknowledge that self-advocacy is often uncomfortable. Quite honestly, I don't like confrontation. I'm not always good about asking for help (my wife calls this "male-itis"). Although these feelings are natural, they are not generally productive.

A college graduate with learning disabilities who has had a successful experience with DS should have acquired knowledge and skills beyond those learned from books and classes. If DS has done its job, the graduating student will have a repertoire of survival skills to use in the world beyond college. Self-advocacy is the engine that drives successful adaptation to adult life and responsibilities.

The prognosis for individuals with learning disabilities who are not effective self-advocates is bleak. Adult life tends to be much more satisfying for individuals who have a sense of themselves as independent and autonomous. A lack of self-advocacy skills may lead to feelings of dependence and insufficiency.

What can young adults with learning disabilities do if they need to improve their self-advocacy skills outside of school? A number of training programs, many of them residential, exist to help young adults with learning disabilities adjust to the demands of independent adulthood. Learning Disabilities Research and Training Center (LDR&TC) has a website full of resources for adults with learning disabilities (http://www.rit.edu/~easi/pubs/ldnoelbw.htm), which includes descriptions of many of these programs. College graduates with learning disabilities who need a boost more typically get involved with adult support groups. The LDR&TC website lists a number of these groups. Marin Puzzle People in Mill Valley, CA is one of the oldest support groups for adults with learning disabilities, founded by Joanne Hazelton more than 20 years ago. This agency explicitly addresses self-advocacy as a goal. Mark Titus, a former student of mine, founded the Fun Bunch in 1999.

This group, for adults with learning disabilities in the Washington, D.C. area, meets once or twice a month and provides social activities and a supportive environment of peers who've "been there and done that."

Individual counseling offers the most personal approach for improving self-advocacy skills. Specially trained counselors who work on helping clients develop specific behavioral life skills are very effective. Sometimes, adults with learning disabilities are able to connect with this kind of counseling and training through their local department of vocational rehabilitation or rehabilitative services. Others use private providers, whose services are sometimes covered by health insurance. To find counseling that focuses on developing skills such as self-advocacy, you might start by going back to local school psychologists, particularly those who conduct evaluations for learning disabilities; they usually know counselors and therapists who specialize in working with older adolescents and adults with learning disabilities. Many high schools have transition specialists or coordinators; these teachers generally have a great sense of all kinds of community resources including counseling.

## Stand Up for Your Right(s) — Again!

When students leave high school and get to college, everything changes. When students leave college and enter the workplace, everything changes again. As in college, individuals with learning disabilities have rights, but not entitlements, in the workplace. Unlike college, however, there is no DS office waiting or actively seeking to help out adults with learning disabilities.

The ADA does protect people with disabilities from employment discrimination as long as they are otherwise qualified for a job. For people with obvious disabilities, this concept isn't too hard to understand. The disability part— let's say using a wheelchair—cannot prevent someone from getting a job as a salesperson, as long as that person is qualified at sales. Ramps may have to be installed, the register may have to be lowered, but denying this individual the right to work solely on the basis of the disability is a form of illegal discrimination, a violation of civil rights.

Learning disabilities are less apparent than physical disabilities. In many situations, the impact of a learning disability is fuzzy and difficult to assess. For example, I have a friend with learning disabilities who has real difficulty with math, especially basic computation. He got a job as a bank teller (probably not a great choice in the goodness-of-fit department). By the end of the first week, his ledger was a mess. Banks don't like it when tellers give away money by mistake, and he was canned. Was he otherwise qualified? That is, would he have been a competent teller if the bank had provided a reasonable accommodation? As you might imagine, "otherwise qualified" becomes pretty tricky to determine for people with learning disabilities. In this case, the bank could probably make a good case that having good computational skills is an essential element of effective job performance, so my friend was out of luck.

Adults with learning disabilities do have rights, but

not unlimited rights. The ADA merely ensures equal access to work opportunities. Self-advocacy is most effective when the individual with learning disabilities has credibility. Things can almost always be worked out without resorting to legal recourse or threats. Success or failure is up to the individual. The ability to plan and set goals, the willingness and ability to self-advocate effectively, and the determination to succeed, even when the odds seem stacked are characteristics of people who stand up for their rights.

I cannot overstate the importance of not seeing oneself as a victim. Self-advocating isn't about asking for handouts or special favors because of a lack of capability. An individual with learning disabilities should avoid the trap of learned helplessness. Toward the end of this book, I will describe how various adults with learning disabilities have become successful. You will find that these individuals have reframed their learning disabilities. As successful adults they have managed not only to accept who they are, but also to understand that their learning styles are not really deficient, just different. They are equally aware of their strengths and their weaknesses. They see themselves as unique, not weak, individuals. They develop plans for how to accommodate their learning disabilities, and even make their so called learning disabilities work for them. People with learning disabilities who advocate for themselves should hold their heads up high. They are not being helpless. They are taking care of themselves—independently. And that's the whole idea.

## Making a First Impression That's not the Last Impression

Roy's life was not easy. Even with all the resources available to him at a private high school for students with learning disabilities, he had barely managed to graduate. By the time he was in his early 20s, his life was marked more by frustration than by the positive goals and hopes of most young men. Bouncing around from one minimum-wage, dead-end job to another, he was living at home with his mom, mainly to have enough money to keep up payments on his car, his one source of pleasure and pride. Why couldn't Roy get his life together? Consider the impression he made in an interview for a job as a stereo installer. He didn't like filling out applications—who does?—but he made a point of telling that to the secretary. He took a long time with the application, being extra careful because he was positive he could do this job. He handed in the application expecting that the boss would let him know immediately that he'd been hired. When told that he'd be notified later, he got exasperated and upset. He scowled and said that he couldn't just sit around and wait to be called. Guess who didn't get the job?

Roy might have been a pretty good stereo installer, but he never got the chance to find out. First impressions are critical. Roy, and many other adults with learning disabilities like him, often make lousy first impressions.

In the workplace, the first impression is usually made at the interview. Consequently, knowing how to come across well in interview situations is a highly desirable skill. Conversely, the "Roy technique" usually gets the response,

"Don't let the door hit ya where the dog should have bit ya"—or something like that. Many colleges and universities have programs, typically career services, that help students develop sound interviewing techniques. In some cases, the DS office may offer similar training.

But let's assume that a young man or woman with learning disabilities has graduated college but never read this book—or at least has some good reason for being uncomfortable and insecure about interviewing for a job. All the suggestions I made earlier about building self-advocacy skills still apply. Training programs, support groups, and individual counseling are potentially great resources for improving interviewing skills.

The best way to learn about how to present well in an interview is through experience. If you want to learn to play a sport, you can read up on the rules, you can do drills, you can practice technique, but ultimately, the best thing is to play the game. Individuals who want to get experience interviewing can practice by applying to all sorts of jobs and going on interviews– without worrying about getting the job. I encourage interviewing for jobs that are not in the person's area of interest or expertise. Learning to sound informed, especially when you're not, is an essential inter-viewing skill. Or, as I used to remind myself before a par-ticularly demanding interview, "If you can't dazzle 'em with brilliance, baffle 'em with ...." The point is that the objective is to get experience, not to get a job. With every "fake" interview, confidence, comfort, and skills grow. And if a job offer is made, well, maybe this is the start of a whole new career!

## Social Skills in the Workplace

Underlying so many of Roy's problems were his poor social skills. It was hard to pinpoint exactly where he had social problems. Perhaps it was the lack of a handshake when meeting someone in a professional situation, or too little (or too much) eye contact. In some social situations, it was hard to tell if he was paying attention to what the other person was saying. He'd abruptly change the subject, focus on irrelevant details, or not quite get the overall gist of the conversation.

Other characteristics associated with learning disabilities may contribute to social skills deficits. Roy's problems with impulse control and distractibility (often associated with an attention deficit), reasoning (particularly in understanding cause and effect), defining problems, and evaluating consequences combined to sour both social and professional interactions. To make matters worse, Roy gave the impression that he was totally unaware of his shortcomings. As a result, he tended to blame other people for his problems, frequently behaving belligerently, as was demonstrated in his interview to be a stereo installer. As you may imagine, Roy's lack of social skills could make other people feel uncomfortable; it was so difficult to get a read on him. It would be easy to dismiss Roy as obnoxious and odd, but his behavior was not the result of psychological or emotional imbalances. Instead, he had problems with social skills, those subtle, complex codes that mediate our interactions with others.

In an article I wrote for *Linkages* (Vol. 2, No. 2), the newsletter of the National Adult Literacy and Learning Disabilities Center, I explain why a number of adults with learning disabilities have difficulties with social skills. In some cases, problems with processing language put a person at risk for not understanding everything that is said, or not being able to express what he or she really means. Moreover, social skills are learned; we are not born with the knowledge to stand about three feet apart from others in social settings. We learn through observation and through the consequences, both good and bad, of our social behavior. We learn to interpret nonverbal communication such as facial expressions, tone of voice, and gestures. We learn to make eye contact, to pay attention and express interest, to wait our turn, to respond appropriately. We learn how far or how near to stand to each other, and we learn how to gauge others' reactions to us.

We also learn that the conventions of social intercourse are fluid and malleable. What's appropriate in one situation, or with one person, may not be appropriate in another. Although we may bumble and stumble here and there, learning how to act appropriately with others comes naturally to most of us, more or less. We may not have been formally taught social skills, but we become adept through incidental learning. Many adults with learning disabilities have not been able to pick up on a lot of this "incidental learning."

Why are social skills so important? First, they tend to be critical for developing meaningful and satisfying relationships. Many adults with learning disabilities complain that they have less than satisfying social lives, are lonely, feel rejected, and because they often don't know why they have these problems, are often frustrated and angry. In addition to the personal implications, social skills are absolutely essential for success in the workplace. Research indicates that job success is associated more with good social skills than with vocational competence. To put it another way, you might have the most skilled mechanic in town working at your garage, but if she(!) is constantly getting into fights with other employees, giving a lot of lip to supervisors, and alienating customers, she will probably not last long at her job. Conversely, we all know someone who isn't the world's greatest worker but is just so darned friendly and charming that it doesn't really hurt to keep him on the roster.

We've seen how poor social skills can ruin an interview. Now, let's imagine that Roy somehow gets through an interview and lands a job. His supervisor asks him to fill an order. Roy doesn't feel like it, but instead of keeping quiet and doing as he's told, he impulsively responds that it's a real pain in the ass to fill orders. As his supervisor tells him the order, he's not really paying attention. Consequently, he has trouble filling it. When he asks (or demands) a coworker for help, the coworker isn't interested and doesn't know the order. Instead of letting it slide, Roy makes an inappropriate comment. When Roy turns in the incorrect order, his supervisor admonishes him. Roy doesn't like to be criticized (who does?) but rather than sucking it up, he launches into a tirade of why the company and everyone who works for it are terrible. You can guess how this story ends.

Of all the challenges facing individuals with learning disabilities, developing more proactive and positive social skills may be the most difficult, particularly for those who really do have difficulties with processing nonverbal social interaction. It's very hard to change your behavior when you're not even aware of how you behave. Additionally, by the time they are adults, individuals with learning disabilities who have had social skills difficulties throughout their lives carry a lot of baggage. A lifetime of being teased, ridiculed, rejected, isolated, and lonely may have irreparable effects. The ensuing anger and frustration with oneself and the world get in the way of having positive motivation to change.

On the other hand, most adults with learning disabilities, especially those who have made it through college or university, have not had such nightmarish experiences. In many cases, they have excellent social skills. I have known many people with learning disabilities who found that their social skills were their greatest strength and compensation. They charmed their way through school, and they wound up being successful adults who charm their way through life. As a noted colleague once said, they are destined to become politicians—or con artists. The majority of adults with learning disabilities fall somewhere in the middle of this spectrum.

The pathway to improving social skills is similar to previous suggestions regarding self-advocacy and interviewing. Treatment programs, support groups, individual counseling, and networking offer many options. Numerous national, regional, and local organizations for adults with learning disabilities such as the Learning Disabilities Association of America (LDA—www.ldaamerica.org), the Association on Higher Education and Disability (AHEAD—www.ahead.org), and the National Network of Learning Disabled Adults (to name but a few) offer networks of services and support that may help adults with learning disabilities understand and overcome many of their social skills deficits.

Individual counseling focusing on behaviorally-oriented therapy appears to be effective in helping people modify, change and improve social skills. Finally, trusted friends and loved ones might help. Sensitive yet objective feedback, when requested, can help some adults with learning disabilities recognize and even change social behaviors. Taking the initiative to change isn't always an easy step, but it's the best way to start improving social skills. Once again, self-advocacy is the engine that drives the process. Adults with learning disabilities cannot rely on others to figure out their problems for them. They have to stand up for themselves.

# Finding the Road to Success When You Can't Read the Directions

### Successful Adults With Learning Disabilities

When I was a graduate student at the University of New Orleans, I was lucky enough to meet Dr. Paul Gerber who became my professional mentor and best friend. Having a mentor often plays a critical role in finding success in life. Paul gave me many gifts, particularly by including me in a major research project on successful adults with learning disabilities. Along with another professor, Rick Ginsberg, who also became my good friend, Paul and I set out to discover how some adults with learning disabilities managed to become extremely successful in their careers in spite of all the challenges they faced. With a team of researchers, we conducted more than seventy in-depth interviews with very successful adults with learning disabilities. Eventually, we presented our research in a book, *Exceeding Expectations: Successful Adults with Learning Disabilities* (1997, PRO-ED).

In conducting our research, we spoke with adults with learning disabilities who were successful doctors, lawyers, professors, professionals of all stripes, and especially entrepreneurs. What struck us most upon hearing their stories were the remarkable similarities in how they became successful. From these interviews we developed a model of vocational success, which highlighted mindsets or attitudes these people had developed about how to live their lives, as well as the behaviors and actions they put into place to achieve their goals.

The following three attitudes or mindsets (we called them "internal decisions") emerged from their stories:

1. Every individual we interviewed had the *desire* to be successful. Several talked about being "on fire" to succeed. This desire often arose from an "I'll show you" reaction to being told "you can't do it."

2. All the participants in our study were extremely goal oriented. They set specific goals for themselves and broke each goal down into manageable steps in order to tackle one at a time.

3. Each developed a personal understanding of his or her individual learning disabilities and reframed this knowledge into a productive and positive affirmation. One successful adult captured the essence of reframing the learning disabilities experience by saying, "I learned to accept who I am, what I can

do, what I cannot do, who I should not try to be, and who I should try to be" (*Exceeding Expectations*, p. 172).

This level of self-actualization is the foundation for success, but in order to be productive, actions or behaviors must follow. These successful adults with learning disabilities took the following actions:

1. They worked hard—harder than anyone else—a quality that we labeled as persistence.

2. They meshed their goal orientation with finding goodness-of-fit in their careers. That is, they found jobs they loved that maximized their strengths and minimized their weaknesses.

3. They developed special strategies and coping mechanisms that compensated for their learning disabilities. We called this approach "learned creativity."

4. They established positive and supportive interpersonal relationships, ranging from mentors to support staff in the workplace, a phenomenon we termed "favorable social ecologies."

By putting all of these components together, the adults we spoke with took control of their lives. Mind you, they did not become control freaks who need to have everything their way. Instead, they recognized that being in control has more to do with having personal autonomy, self-directedness, and accountability. These qualities share an interactive dynamic with self-advocacy. Nobody gives you control over your own life. You have to take it. These adults became successful because they took charge of their lives, which means they advocated for themselves.

CS

# Accommodations in the Workplace

## What the Law Says

The ADA is quite clear when it comes to protecting the rights of individuals with disabilities in the workplace. For adults with learning disabilities, the two most relevant issues are non-discrimination and accommodation. An employer cannot discriminate against an individual on the basis of a learning disability in terms of hiring, treatment on the job, or firing. This does not mean that persons with learning disabilities will always be hired, treated well, and never fired. The law employs the term "otherwise qualified," meaning that, aside from the disability, the individual has the necessary skills and qualifications for the job. Consequently, in order to be protected by the ADA, an individual with (learning) disabilities must make a case for being qualified. Some cases are obvious, but more often than not, the situation gets murky with learning disabilities. If a person with severe reading disabilities (who has been able to make it through college using books on tape) seeks employment as a proofreader, can that person be considered otherwise qualified, or does the disability itself unequivocally prevent the person from being qualified?

To a large extent, the answer depends on whether the person can perform the essential functions of the job with reasonable accommodations. In most cases, barriers to successful job performance can be overcome. Again, these issues are relatively clear when it comes to most physical or sensory disabilities, although debate may ensue over the "reasonableness" of an accommodation. An able employee who is deaf may prefer to have an interpreter at all times, but it may not be reasonable for a small firm to pay for a full-time interpreter, especially if the interpreter's salary is higher than the employee's.

## Determining Reasonable Accommodations

What types of accommodations help otherwise qualified individuals with learning disabilities perform the essential functions of a job? In school, most tests are designed to measure what students know, not how fast they can answer the questions. Consequently, extended time for testing is reasonable because it allows students with learning disabilities who may process more slowly to show what they indeed know. In the workplace, extended time may interfere with the essential function of the job. A newspaper reporter with learning disabilities probably cannot make a case for extended time to file breaking news reports. Talk about yesterday's headlines!

In many cases, fairly simple and inexpensive accommodations can help otherwise qualified persons with learning disabilities be successful in the workplace. As with most responsibilities, creating the most effective work environment requires self-advocacy skills. Employers are unlikely to initiate accommodations, no matter how empathetic they may be. They're not mind readers. It's the responsibility of employees with learning disabilities to communicate with their supervisors and/or human resources—and not just to communicate that there may be a problem. A solution is now required. The workplace does not have a DS office with trained professionals who can determine what kinds of accommodations are called for. The expert is now the adult with learning disabilities.

Accommodating the workplace for adult employees with learning disabilities is a much trickier proposition than accommodating students in college. There are no standard or typical accommodations. The Job Accommodations Network (JAN), contracted by the U. S. Department of Labor, offers sample workplace accommodations for employees with learning disabilities (http://www.jan.wvu.edu). Many of the suggestions refer to the same kinds of assistive technology discussed in Chapter Two, such as books on tape, reading machines, laptops, specialized software, calculators (standard or talking), etc.

Similar to the situation in college, many accommodations in the workplace can be positively lo-tech yet highly effective, such as color-coded manuals, files, or ledgers; locator dots on keyboards; and workspace partitions for reducing distractions. The website also provides brief case studies of accommodations in the workplace, ranging from being assigned to only one task at a time, to having a temporary job coach. Learning Disabilities Worldwide's website offers a clear summary of what the ADA does and does not offer adults with learning disabilities in the workplace on its website at http://www.ldam.org/ldinformation/adults/504_gotthelf.html.

Tony, an adult with learning disabilities who had made a fortune as a waiter in high school, told me that he had to develop a special coding system in order to write down orders. He was a wonderful self-advocate, and he worked with the chef, cooks, and manager to develop his system. Because he had great interpersonal skills as a waiter, his coworkers were happy to accommodate him.

Nevertheless, we live in a culture that is still distrustful of the very existence of learning disabilities. I'd like to say it isn't so, but whether or not an employee with learning disabilities can negotiate accommodations depends largely on the culture of the workplace. Tony's boss was open, willing, and flexible, which made for a win-win situation. Other employers will not be so forthcoming, and a legal battle over issues such as flexible hours and extended time, additional technical support, lighter reading and writing loads, may not hold up in court. Even in a potentially accommodating workplace, someone such as Roy could probably manage to sour an employer's best intentions to be accommodating.

In my experience, most employees with learning disabilities don't think the ADA has much relevance. They are usually aware that it was important to them in college, but in the workplace they see it as ensuring access for persons with physical or sensory disabilities. As part of a research project, I asked seven young adults with learning disabilities whether they had ever brought up the ADA on the job. They all said they had not. In the upcoming "Tips for Students" section, I will discuss some of the pros and cons of disclosing one's learning disabilities on the job, which de facto invokes the ADA.

# There's More to Life Than Work

## What Is Success?

When Paul, Rick, and I were developing our study on highly successful adults with learning disabilities, we knew that we needed to come up with a definition of vocational success that would be universally accepted. We selected five criteria: income level, education level, prominence in one's field, job satisfaction, and job classification (i.e., highly professional). In order to qualify as highly successful, candidates had to score at the top in four of the five categories. This seemed to be a good system for ensuring that readers and critics would agree that our participants were highly successful. However, as I have examined my own life, I've developed a somewhat different perspective.

I don't make a great deal of money. I'm not famous. I don't have wall full of commendations, citations, and awards. But I'm happy. I do feel that I'm a success. Why? On my office wall is a beautiful framed graphic of a poem by Ralph Waldo Emerson, a gift from a student, Jen, who struggled and lost direction, but upon working with me, went on to graduate. I knew that she appreciated the time we had spent together. In the end, I appreciated it just as much as she did. Jen's choice of these words helped me reframe my very notions of success:

To laugh often and much;
To win the respect of intelligent people
and the affection of children;
To earn the appreciation of honest critics
and endure the betrayal of false friends;
To appreciate beauty,
to find the best in others;
To leave the world a bit better,
whether by a healthy child, a garden patch
or a redeemed social condition;
To know even one life has breathed easier
because you have lived.
This is to have succeeded. [1]

Have you touched someone? Are you trying to make the world a better place? Maybe you're not sure. Jimmy Stewart as George Bailey in *It's a Wonderful Life* didn't think his life meant much until Clarence showed him a world without George Bailey. When George understood that he had touched so many lives in so many ways, he realized that he was happy. He was a success.

So maybe it's not wealth, power, and prestige that define success. But don't be lulled into thinking that with the right reframing, success just happens. You do have to work for it. In the book *Tuesdays with Morrie* by Mitch Albom, Morrie presents a thoughtful to-do list:

1. Love your family and connect with others to love and care about.

---

[1] Some controversy exists as to whether Emerson is the true author. Bessie Stanley may have been the source (http://www.transcendentalists.com/success.htm).

2. Find a career that has meaning for you.

3. Contribute to the greater good of your community.

The key to making it happen? Self-advocacy. To get love, give love. To find a meaningful career, take stock of yourself and put your plans into action. To contribute, get off your butt. Now you're on the road to success.

## Life 101

I was pretty naïve when I graduated from college at the age of twenty-one. I had always been a good student. I don't think I ever failed a test. I thought I had my act to-gether—but I was woefully under prepared. Not only did I not know how to deal with failure, I had no idea that no one goes through life without failing. I didn't know what I didn't know. By the time I was twenty-five, I was quickly becoming an expert in failure. I had a failed music career, a failed marriage, and a failed bank account. What was worse, I didn't know how to cope. Instead of persevering, I initially made matters worse by drinking, losing control of my car, and smashing into a concrete abutment at sixty miles per hour. I had hit the wall, literally as well as figuratively.

The fact that I lived was nothing short of a miracle. The insurance adjuster did not even come to the hospital for several days because after looking at my car, he assumed I was dead. I was down so low, I had no place to go but up. I really don't know how I turned things around, but I did learn that I could not give up on myself. I also discovered that I could learn and grow stronger because of failure.

Persistence was forced on me. I had no choice. I strongly recommend against emulating my spiritual journey (at least the car part). Instead, try to put failure in its proper perspective. No one succeeds without taking risks and failing. If nothing else, failing is integral to figuring out what works through the process of elimination. No one will remember the times we stumble along the way, as long as we make it to the finish line.

Thomas Edison may have been the biggest failure of all time. He also was a firm believer in the importance of failure. Failure was what led him to success. Once, when he was working on developing a better battery, a discouraged assistant came up to him and suggested that Mr. Edison must be ready to quit after having performed some 50,000 tests without success. "You must be pretty downhearted with the lack of progress," the assistant said. Edison replied, "Downhearted? We've made a lot of progress. At least we know 50,000 things that won't work!" (http://www.homeschoollearning.com/units/unit_09-06-01.shtml)

Persons with learning disabilities may actually have a leg up on people without learnind disabilities when it comes to knowing how to deal with failure. For so many, school is a constant barrage of hearing about what they are not good at, about what they cannot do, about failure. Almost all of the successful adults with learning disabilities I've encountered cite dealing with failure as the backbone to their success. They learned not to give up. They learned that failure can lead to new and better ideas or ways of doing things. One of our participants said, "The learning disability positively affected my success.... I learned to persist, to deal with pain and frustration" (*Exceeding Expectations*, p. 110).

When it comes to understanding the meaning of life, I hardly qualify as an expert. If there were stock value in my shares of mistakes, I'd be a millionaire. On the other hand, I've probably learned more in the school of hard knocks than I did in my doctoral program. I may not always know what to do, but I have a pretty good sense of what not to do, and it didn't even take 50,000 tests without success for me to learn it!

As much as there is to be said for ambition and career success, I've never heard of anyone taking that final breath on their deathbed and say, "I wish I'd spent more time at the office." As with many professionals, I sometimes wonder if I have made the most of my career. I could have/should have written more books by now. I could have/should have reached a more prestigious position. I could have/should have made more money. I could have done more, could be doing more, but I really have no regrets. When I get home at the end of the day, I return to my top priority, my family. I may think other things in life are really important, but if one of my kids is sick, upset, or struggling; if my wife and I are going through a rough patch; if my mother needs my help.... it's obvious what really matters.

# Tips for Students

## To Disclose or Not to Disclose — That Is the Question

Remember that just as no one could force you to identify yourself as a person with learning disabilities when you were in college, you're not required to tell anyone in the workplace that you have learning disabilities. In situations where it's irrelevant, disclosure is hardly necessary. However, you may find that your learning disabilities have more of an impact on your life after school than you thought. It may be worthwhile to disclose in many situations.

Interestingly, I conducted a number of interviews recently with young adults, asking them whether they disclose their learning disabilities at work, in postsecondary education (usually two-year or trade schools), in the community, or with family. While some had disclosed during their postsecondary education, few had brought up their learning disabilities at work, and none talked about it in the community. They were all comfortable talking about their learning disabilities with their families, but it was not a topic that came up very often.

I hesitate to offer a rule of thumb about identifying yourself as an adult with learning disabilities. It's not something you want to hide, and it's definitely not something to be ashamed of. But it's not something that you really need to shout out to the world either. I have some issues with depression and take an anti-depressant. I'm not ashamed and have no need to hide this, but I don't go around telling people I'm on drugs (so to speak) every chance I get. I try to share this part of me when it's relevant. I meet many students who struggle with emotional issues and who may be on medication. Sharing this part of myself with them may help to create trust and comfort.

Your comfort level with yourself will have much to do with when, where, and why you disclose your learning disabilities. The question to ask is, "Is it relevant?" The answer to this question is often unclear. Just because you think your reading disability is irrelevant to your career as an accountant, mixing up "receipt" with "recipe" on a tax form could lead to an audit (not to be confused with the German car). On the other hand, you may feel your difficulty with computation will prevent you from doing data entry, only to find out that data entry means keeping a log of your phone calls.

In most cases, I would not recommend disclosing learning disabilities in the job application/interview process. Every now and then a moving story about overcoming learning disabilities may sell in an interview, but the applicant had better be reading the prospective employer wisely. If it's clear that the learning disabilities will have a direct, negative impact on your ability to do the work, you might want to think twice about this chosen career. Finding the right fit is probably more useful than being a "LD crusader."

There are learning disabilities activists who topple controversial policies, settle workplace issues, and remind us that adults with learning disabilities don't always get a fair shake. They are effective self-advocates who have become group-advocates. This is a noble calling, but not one that I'd recommend for most people. I subscribe to the "pick your battles" philosophy. Adults with learning disabilities need to be effective self-advocates, but they don't need to wear their disabilities on their sleeves.

### *Pick Your Battles*

Most of this book has offered advice on how to self-advocate and stand up for yourself. I also believe in the adage, "moderation in all things." The most effective approach to self-advocacy is tempered by a realization that not every battle is worth fighting. By picking fights indiscriminately, you may undermine your very ability to self-advocate successfully.

Remember our friend, Roy, the would-be stereo installer who did not exactly know *How to Make Friends and Influence People*, to use the title of a famous book by Dale Carnegie. Among Roy's self-imposed difficulties, he did not know when to keep his mouth shut. You may find it ironic that a book about self-advocacy suggests backing off, but consider the alternative. You would not want Roy in your face all the time. You'd find him annoying and obnoxious. And when it came time to deal with a real, legitimate issue, he'd be like the boy who cried wolf. You'd ignore him.

No guide exists to tell you when is the right time to speak up and when is the right time to hold your tongue. Instead, you need to analyze several factors:

- What is the social/cultural environment? Are you comfortable talking about your learning disabilities and needs with others? Are those others comfortable? The more open and accepting the environment, the easier it will be to speak up, but even so, it's not open season. Even your strongest supporters will back off if you needlessly harangue them.

- What are your needs? If a reasonable accommodation is absolutely critical to being able to do a job, the need to self-advocate wins out, even in an inhospitable environment. Conversely, if the issue isn't critical, particularly if you can manage on your own, leave it alone.

- What is your reputation? Are you valued? Can people count on you? Do you always do your best? If so, others will be willing to listen to you and take you seriously. And if you're a slacker.... what do you think?

### If You Do What You Love, You'll Love What You Do

Perhaps you've heard the advice, "Make your avocation your vocation, and you'll always be happy." Successful adults with learning disabilities have said that this was a key component to their achievements. As a person with learning disabilities, finding goodness-of-fit means considering more than just your passion. You need to be acutely aware of your strengths and weaknesses, probably even more so than students without learning disabilities. No matter how much I might love NASCAR—the smell of burning rubber, the roar of a 1960s muscle car, *Grand Theft Auto*—I wouldn't fare well as a mechanic. I might have dreamt about working in the pit at Daytona all my life, but it would be a disaster – literally. One summer I worked as a carpenter's assistant.

Just before he fired me, my boss said, "You'd hurt yourself pushing a broom. The only thing you oughtta push is a pencil, and even then you'll probably hurt yourself." How do you make sure that what you love to do is also what you're good at doing? In a sense, it's a constant process of re-framing. Reflect on how your strengths and weaknesses fit with your interests. In the case of Bob, the dentist, he real-ized that he could not make it through medical school. He reframed his ambition of being a doctor into being a dentist. He now does what he loves and loves what he does. You should also explore your interests. There may be something to be said for knowing where you're going in life from the get-go (Donald Trump was selling apartment buildings in college; Howard Stern played disc jockey when he was six). However, there's an equally strong case to be made for the "undecideds." College is the opportunity of a lifetime to explore interests and possible career paths—through classes, internships, career services, informal discussions with pro-fessors and students, on and off campus employment, and sometimes just through meeting the right people or net-working. After college, don't be afraid to explore and assess your interests, particularly if you feel that you're not on the right road. Increasingly, people are changing careers several times throughout their adult lives. Be aware that there is a fine balance between finding yourself and endlessly bounc-ing from one dead-end job to the next. In some cases, finding a new career path will require additional education or training. It's a commitment. But if you find that goodness-of-fit, if you find a career that you love and you're good at, it's worth the extra blood, sweat, and tears.

# Tips for Parents

## *They Grow Up So Fast — Or Not Fast Enough*

Back off. Let me say it again. Back off. Yes, your kids are still kids. You're still the parent and know so much more. But once your children have finished school, or are twenty-one, or are working, it's time to let go. If your kids listened to you when they were growing up, they probably got it. If they didn't listen to you then, they probably won't start now. Of course, they'll come to you for advice, and you should give it. But keep the helicopter in mothballs.

Would you have wanted your mom or dad butting in at college, sitting down with professors to explain what you needed? Believe me, most professors don't want that either. Now think about the workplace. Don't storm into your child's place of employment to demand accommodations or adjustments. If you think this doesn't work well with a professor, wait until you try it with the boss. It doesn't matter if the law is on your side. Fighting your child's battles does not help healthy adult development. You might humiliate and marginalize your young adult into permanent childhood.

You will support your child most effectively by listening rather than doing. You may find that situations occur for your child in the workplace or social circles that are eerie flashbacks to elementary school. Don't be surprised if you feel the same as you did years ago – angry, upset, disappointed, confused, and most of all, hurting for your child. You may even share your feelings with your child. But don't act on them.

## *Keeping the Empty Nest Empty*

When I was in my twenties, I wanted to get as far away from my parents as I could. In the last twenty years, we've witnessed a new phenomenon where young adults move back home after finishing school. Young adults from all walks of life are trying to retie apron strings. Almost sixty percent of twenty-two to twenty-four-year olds are living at home. Most are single, and probably not increasing their chances of finding a mate while living with mom and dad. There are good reasons why adult children return home — housing costs, debt, unemployment, underemployment, and divorce. Young adults with learning disabilities may be even more vulnerable to these circumstances. It's hard to turn away your kid in these circumstances. Perhaps nothing is wrong with providing a little temporary help to get them on their feet. The problems begin when the help isn't so tempo-rary. There's a big difference between having your twenty-three-year old spend a couple of months at home getting it together compared to a thirty-five-year old whose creature comforts at home seem to make up for a dead-end job.

What can you do to keep your adult child with learn-ing disabilities out of the house? Most of the answer lies in upbringing — territory for Dr. Spock or Dr. Phil. However, I'd like to share some insights about parenting from successful adults with learning disabilities. In one way or another, many successful adults with learning disabilities credit their positive characteristics to their upbringing, particularly in the support they received from their parents. So many kids with learning disabilities face a hostile and skeptical world filled with hurt and humiliation. A college student once told me that he remembered playing with ants on the elementary school playground because no one would play with him, and then being attacked for being so weird.

For many children with learning disabilities who have gone on to have satisfying adult lives, parents have been the shelter from the storm. For that alone, many adults are grateful. More importantly, many successful adults with learning disabilities knew that their parents believed in them, no matter what barrage of negativity assaulted them. "My mother never gave up on me," one student recalled. "She explained that it never hurt to keep trying. She just refused to believe all those people who called me a dummy or re-tard" (*Exceeding Expectations*, p.187). Their parents instilled confidence, desire, and determination: "I had an unbeliev-able mother. She made me believe that I could do any-thing.... She was supportive and never made me feel inad-equate" (*Exceeding Expectations*, p.45).

The best advice I can give to you comes from suc-cessful adults with learning disabilities. They've been there, done that, and now they're parents too. A good friend, Ken, who's a celebrity psychologist — and an adult with learning disabilities — puts it this way: "Support your kids. Give them every bit of confidence you can give them. They are different and they need to know that that's OK.... Let them do the things they are good at without forcing skills that will never be mastered no matter how long you spend on them. If you stifle their creativity, you've damaged them for life" (*Exceed-ing Expectations*, p.202).

A story that still brings tears to my eyes comes from my friend, Coller, a successful dermatologist from a prestigious medical family—and an adult with learning disabilities. She tells of the constant battles she fought to survive school, eventually turning into a "bad kid," which she thought was better than being seen as stupid. Her parents never gave up, never backed off, and never let her down. Coller will look you in the eye and say, "When you have parents who love you and believe in you so much, you just don't let them down." Take that, Dr. Phil.

# Tips for Guidance Counselors

### Career Planning in High School for the College-Bound

More than one successful adult with learning disabilities that I know has recounted horror stories about high school guidance counselors. Can you imagine a counselor calling a student a "J.I.T." — janitor in training? Those are the exact words one of the successful adults interviewed in *Exceeding Expectations* heard from his guidance counselor in high school. It's hard to believe that a professional educator would dismiss a student with such utter disregard and contempt. This kind of ignorance about students with learning disabilities is hopefully a relic of a bygone era. Nevertheless, an ill-timed, insensitive, or misinformed judgment may have a devastating effect on a student that lasts a lifetime. Conversely, a guidance counselor who understands the untapped potential of students with learning disabilities may catalyze a future of boundless success.

I have dedicated this book to students with learning disabilities who plan to go to college or university. Your relationships with these students will focus on preparing them in high school to make that transition. This does not mean that you should neglect career planning with college-bound students. Like their peers who will not attend college, these students need career counseling beginning in high school, if not earlier.

In some cases, a sense of career interest drives the most basic decisions about what kind of college to attend. A high school student with learning disabilities who loves graphic design will do better in a college that offers a program in that field. The student may ultimately choose a different focus, but without the opportunity to pursue one's interest, the entire college experience may be filled with second guessing, "what ifs", and in some cases, dissatisfaction that leads to dropping out. Similarly, the high school student who knows he or she wants to be a doctor can begin taking required pre-med courses right off the bat in college.

Career planning for students with learning disabilities can be somewhat different than for other students. Pay close attention to the concept of goodness-of-fit. That is, individuals with learning disabilities usually have some weaknesses that may make certain careers quite unlikely. You have to walk a fine line between gently guiding students toward their areas of strength without stomping out their dreams. Helping students with learning disabilities reframe their limitations plays a key role. We all have things that we are not good at doing. Conversely, we all have strengths. We've got to recognize both. The successful adults with learning disabilities that my colleagues and I studied emphasized over and over again that success came from recognizing, accepting, and understanding their learning disabilities, and then planning their lives based on their strengths, weaknesses and needs—the reframing process.

Bob, the dentist, provides an excellent example of someone who reframed his notion of his learning disabilities to see the positives without blinding himself to the reality that medical school was not in his future. Instead, he redirected his goal orientation and found goodness-of-fit in dental school.

The more that you help your students with learning disabilities discover who they are, the more you will be guiding them on the path to fulfilling careers. Reviewing documentation from evaluations with high school students will get them thinking about their strengths, weaknesses, and needs – not only as they apply to college, but also in relation to possibilities for careers. The counseling skills that you already possess will facilitate this journey.

### *Getting Your Students to Think About the Next Seventy Years*

Talking to teenagers about what they'll be doing for the rest of their lives usually results in blank stares and slack jaws. For most, adulthood is a strange and foreign land that they cannot imagine inhabiting. But you can do a great deal to help students with learning disabilities develop skills that will help them make it in college and beyond.

You can help students build desire, focus on goals, and reframe their notions of themselves and their learning disabilities in a positive and productive way. You can teach students how to be persistent, determine goodness-of-fit, develop learned creativity, and build favorable social ecologies. You can help your students with learning disabilities get in control of their lives now, which gives them a jumpstart on maintaining control of their lives in adulthood.

An astute and dedicated guidance counselor may be the guiding force behind a favorable social ecology for a student with learning disabilities. You may be the person who networks with others who can support your student, including parents, teachers, admissions counselors, and so on. You may be able to impart to your students the importance of working interdependently with others, an increasingly crucial skill in a highly complex and specialized workplace. And you may be that special person, the mentor who inspires, guides, sustains, and celebrates successes with your students while helping them stay the course through failures. You may think that you're only preparing your students for the next step to college; if you help them develop the attitudes, knowledge, and skills that I've discussed, your influence will last a lifetime. By supporting, teaching, and instilling the skills of self-advocacy, you can provide the gift that keeps on giving.

## Resources

Association on Higher Education and Disability. (1997). *Guidelines for documentation of learning disabilities in adolescents and adults.* Columbus, OH: AHEAD and www.ahead.org.

Allard, W. (1987). Keeping learning disabled students in college. *Academic Therapy, 22,* 359-365.

Bender, W. (2002). *Differentiating instruction for students with learning disabilities.* Thousand Oaks, CA: Corwin Press.

Brooks, R. (1999). *Learning disabilities and self-esteem: look what you've done* [Video]. Charlotte, NC: PBS Video.

Brozo, W.G., & Curtis, C.L. (1986). *Coping strategies of four successful learning disabled college students: A case study approach.* College Reading and Learning Assistance Technical Report 86-08, Atlanta, GA: Georgia State University.

Brinckerhoff, L.C., Shaw, S. F., & McGuire, J. M. (1992). Promoting access, accommodations, and independence for college students with learning disabilities. *Journal of Learning Disabilities, 25,* 417-429.

Casbarro, J. (2005). *Test anxiety & what you can do about it: A practical guide for teachers, parents, & kids.* Port Chester, NY: Dude Publishing.

Clark, G.M. (1996). Transition planning assessment for secondary-level students with learning disabilities. *Journal of Learning Disabilities, 29,* 79-92.

Cullen, J.P., Shaw, S.F., & McGuire, J.M. (1996). Practitioner support of self-advocacy among college students with learning disabilities: A comparison of practices and attitudes. *Journal of Postsecondary Education and Disability, 12* (2), 2-15.

Cummings, R., Maddux, C.D., & Casey, J. (2000). Individualized transition planning for students with learning disabilities. *Career Development Quarterly, 49* (1), 60-72.

Dendy, C. (2000). *Teaching teens with ADD and ADHD: A quick reference guide for teachers and parents.* Bethesda, MD: Woodbine House.

Durlak, C.M., Rose, E., & Bursuck, W.D. ( 1994). Preparing high school students with learning disabilities for the transition to postsecondary education: Teaching the skills of self-determination. *Journal of Learning Disabilities, 27,* 51-59.

Ellis, D.B. (2006). Becoming a master student (11th edition). Boston, MA: Houghton Mifflin.

Field, S. (1996). Self-determination instructional strategies for youth with learning disabilities. *Journal of Learning Disabilities, 29,* 40-52.

Field, S., & Hoffman A. (1994). Developing a model for self-determination. *Career Development for Exceptional Individuals, 17,* 159-169.

Flick, G.L. (2000). *How to reach and teach teenagers with ADHD: A step-by-step guide to overcoming difficult behaviors at school and at home.* Wiley, John & Sons, Inc.

Gerber, P.J. (2002). Navigating the beyond-school years: Employment and success for adults with learning disabilities. *Learning Disability and Career Development, 18* (1), 36-44.

Gerber, P.J., & Reiff, H.B. (1991). *Speaking for themselves: Ethnographic interviews with adults with learning disabilities.* Ann Arbor, MI: The University of Michigan Press.

Gerber, P.J., & Reiff, H.B. (Eds.). (1994). *Learning disabilities in adulthood: Persisting problems and evolving issues.* Austin,TX: Pro-Ed.

Gerber, P.J., Reiff, H.B., & Ginsberg, R. (1994). Critical incidents in highly successful adults with learning disabilities. *Journal of Vocational Rehabilitation, 4,* 105-112.

Gerber, P.J., Reiff, H.B., & Ginsberg, R. (1996). Reframing the learning disabilities experience. *Journal of Learning Disabilities, 29,* 98-101, 97.

Guilford Press (Producer). (1999). *Assessing ADHD in the schools* [Video]. New York, NY.

Hatzes, N.M. (1996). Factors contributing to the academic outcomes of university students with learning disabilities. *Dissertation Abstracts International.*

Hatzes, N.M., Reiff, H.B., & Bramel, M.H. (2002). The documentation dilemma: Access and accommodations for postsecondary students with learning disabilities. *Assessment for Effective Intervention, 27* (3), 37-52.

Hughes, C. & Carter, E.W. (2000). *The Transition handbook: Strategies high school teachers use that work!* Baltimore, MD: Paul H. Brookes Publishing.

Jensen, E. (2000). *Different brains, different learners: How to reach the hard to reach.* San Diego, CA: The Brain Store.

Kerka, S. (2002). *Learning disabilities and career development. (Practice application brief no. 20).* Washington, D.C.: Office of Educational Research & Improvement.

Lavoie, R. (2005). *Beyond F.A.T. city* [Video]. Charlotte, NC: PBS Video.

Lavoie, R. (1989). *F.A.T. city: How difficult can this be?* [Video]. Charlotte, NC: PBS Video.

Lavoie, R. (2005). *It's so much work to be your friend* [Video]. Charlotte, NC: PBS Video.

Lavoie, R. (2005). *It's so much work to be your friend.* Chicago, IL: Simon & Schuster.

Lavoie, R. (1994). *Learning disabilities and social skills: Last one picked? first one picked on* [Video]. Charlotte, NC: PBS Video.

Lavoie, R. (2005). *When the chips are down* [Video]. Charlotte, NC: PBS Video.

Levine, M. (2003). *The myth of laziness.* Chicago, IL: Simon & Schuster.

Likoff, L. (2005). *Encyclopedia of careers and vocational guidance,* (Thirteenth Edition). New York, NY: InfoBase Publishing.

Palmer, A. (2006). *Realizing the college dream with autism or asperger syndrome.* Herndon, VA: Jessica Kingsley Publications, Inc.

Phillips, P. (1990). A self-advocacy plan for high school students with learning disabilities: A comparative case study analysis of students', teachers', and parents' perceptions of program effects. *Journal of Learning Disabilities, 23,* 466-471.

Raskind, M.H., Goldberg, R.J., Higgins, E.L., & Herman K.L. (1999). Patterns of change and predictors of success in individuals with learning disabilities: Results from a twenty-year longitudinal study. *Learning Disabilities Research and Practice, 14* (1), 35-49.

Reiff, H.B. (2002). Learning disabilities from the inside out: A program for self-actualization. *Thalamus: Journal of the International Academy for Research in Learning Disabilities, 20* (1), 50-62.

Reiff, H.B. (2004). Reframing the learning disabilities experience redux. *Learning Disabilities Research and Practice, 19* (3), 185-198.

Reiff, H.B., & deFur, S. (1992). Transition for youths with learning disabilities: A focus on developing independence. *Learning Disability Quarterly, 15*, 237-249.

Reiff, H.B., Gerber, P.J., & Ginsberg, R. (1997). *Exceeding expectations: Successful adults with learning disabilities.* Austin, TX: PRO-ED.

Rief, S.F. (2003). *The ADHD book of lists.* Newark, NJ: Wiley, John & Sons, Inc.

Rief, S.F. (2004). *ADHD & LD: Powerful teaching strategies & accommodations* [Video]. Port Chester, NY: National Professional Resources, Inc.

Rief, S.F. & Heimburge, J.A. (1996). *How to reach & teach all students in the inclusive classroom: Ready-to-use strategies, lessons, and activities for teaching students with learning needs.* West Nyack, NY: Center for Applied Research in Education.

Roffman, A.J., Herzog, J.E., & Wershba-Gershon, P.M. (1994). Helping young adults understand their learning disabilities. *Journal of Learning Disabilities, 27*, 413-419.

Rothman, H.R., & Cosden, M. (1995). The relationship between self-perception of a learning disability and achievement, self-concept and social support. *Learning Disability Quarterly, 18*, 203-212.

Sachs, J.J., Iliff, V.W., & Donnelly, R.F. (1987). Oh, ok I'm LD! *Journal of Learning Disabilities, 20*, 92-93.

Siegal, L.M. (2004). *Nolo's IEP guide: Learning disabilities.* Berkley, CA: Nolo.

Seligman, M. (1991). *Learned optimism.* New York: Knopf.

Shulman, S. (1984). Psychotherapeutic issues for the learning disabled adult. *Professional Psychology: Research and Practice, 15*, 856-867.

Smith, S. (2001). *Teach me different! Successful strategies for teaching children who learn differently* [Video]. Charlotte, NC: PBS Video.

Sousa, D.A. (2001). *How the special needs brain learns.* Thousand Oaks, CA: Corwin Press.

Spekman, N.J., Goldberg, R.J., & Herman, K.L. (1993). An exploration of risk and resilience in the lives of individuals with learning disabilities. *Learning Disabilities Research & Practice, 8*, 11-18.

State of the Art, Inc. (2003). *My future my plan: Transition planning resource for life after high school.* Washington, DC.

Strichart, S.S., Mangrum II, C.T., Iannuzzi, P. (2002). *Teaching learning strategies and study skills to students with learning disabilities, ADD, or special needs.* Atlanta, GA: Prentice Hall.

Swanson, H. L., Harris, K.R., Graham, S. (2003). *Handbook of learning disabilities.* New York, NY: Guilford Press.

Swanson, H.L., Hoskyn, M., Lee, C. (1999). *Interventions for students with learning disabilities: A meta-analysis of treatment outcomes.* New York, NY: Guilford Press.

Thomsen, K. (2002). *Building resilient students: Integrating resiliency into what you already know and do.* Thousand Oaks, CA: Corwin Press.

Vogel, S.A., & Adelman, P.B. (1992). The success of college students with learning disabilities: Factors related to educational attainment. *Journal of Learning Disabilities, 25,* 430- 441.

## About the Author

**Henry B. Reiff, Ph.D.**

Henry B. Reiff is Professor of Special Education and Dean of Student Academic Life at McDaniel College in Westminster, MD. He has co-authored three previous books on adolescents and adults with learning disabilities, including *Exceeding Expectations: Successful Adults with Learning Disabilities*, which was selected by the American Library Association as a Top 20 LD resource. He resides in Westminster with his wife, Jacki and their two children.